ENDORSEMENTS

Frank Schattner has written a definitive work on church planting multiplication movements. Spoiler alert: If you want to keep doing church planting business as usual and remain unaware of a present move of God, do not read this book. If you want to press in and see and sense the heart of God in a well researched and passionate form, then settle in and read this book now!

~ **John Jackson, PhD.,**
President of William Jessup University and author of 6 books on leadership and spiritual transformation

This is a book that every God honoring, Bible believing, mission-minded believer, pastor and Seminary teacher should have in his or her library. They should read it with interest and put into practice the principles taught. It will increase your understanding of how to be purpose driven in helping to fulfill the Great Commission in a responsible and dynamic way.

~ **Jim Morris,**
Pioneer Missionary to the Pwo Karen,
Former National Director OMF

We must know where we've been; we must know what we are planting. One without the other is not sufficient. Catalyzing Sustainable Church Multiplication Movements is a practical resource written to help us understand both that the gospel may spread rapidly and with honor among the nations!

**~ J. D. Payne,
Pastor of Church Multiplication, The Church at Brook Hills**

Regardless of your views on CPM, keeping your eyes on the Fruitful Practices as described in Schattner's Wheel model, especially Worldview Transformation, will contribute to seeing the kind of Jesus movement for God's glory we all aim to see. The locals we have introduced this model to find it intuitive and helpful and they are running ahead with it . . . just as it should be!

**~ Jeff Alvarez,
Pioneer Missionary and Strategy Coordinator,
ActBeyond Mission**

Frank is not only a visionary, but is extremely dedicated to the practical "hands on" working out of the vision. He's a practitioner, not a theorist, and writes from that perspective. This book will be of great help to all those who seek to reach the least reached peoples now, rather than later. May the Lord use this book to catalyze church multiplication movements!

**~ Eric Barry,
Vice President of Outreach and Training,
Team Expansion Mission**

The jewel in this little book is the "Wheel model." Frank has a gift of keeping things simple and his wheel model is an excellent tool that can be used in training workers to train others in stating what are the important factors in sustaining a movement. I have used the wheel model to teach individuals and groups. Each time recipients have easily grasped the concepts that I have previously found difficult to convey. Thank you Frank!

~ Andrew Goodman,
Strategy Coordinator for the Shan, Field Director OMF

Frank Schattner's research-based book provides aspects of missiology that are often missed in writings about CPMs. He provides a helpful, comprehensive model of the necessary activities of the worker, but also rightfully recognizes the work of God's Spirit that is necessary at every stage of a movement. Those who long to see sustained CPMs should read this book.

~ Richard Schlitt,
International Director of OMF

Frank Schattner is a refreshing global worker—one of those guys who is driven by the truth of the Gospel and the reality of lost people. This book reflects both "context" and the "reality" of seeing the Gospel spread among the peoples of the earth. You will do well to read it and apply it to your situation—no matter where you serve. May many come to God through Christ because of this little tool.

~ Greg H. Parsons, PhD.,
U.S. Center for World Mission
William Carey International University
Pasadena California
Twitter: parsonsgh

Frank Schattner writes as a practitioner in applying the principles of disciple making movements. He writes out of experience — his own and that of other leading practitioners. Frank also engages the criticisms of church planting movements; specifically the questions of sustainability and quality. Finally Frank proposes a model for sustainable church multiplication movements that is both clear and practical. This is a book that should be read by anyone who takes Jesus at his word when He commanded us to come follow him, and promised to teach us how to make disciples.

~ **Steve Addison,**
Director of MOVE and Author,
"What Jesus Started: Joining
the Movement, Changing the World"

Every disciple maker is interested in planting churches that last. Frank Schattner has made a great contribution to sustainable church planting practice with his very comprehensive model. His emphasis on the role of the Holy Spirit and the importance of vision, training and modeling help to build a solid church planting foundation.

~ **Paul Eshleman,**
CCCI International Vice President,
Networks and Partnerships

The Wheel Model opens great windows of creativity and connectivity for *Catalyzing Sustainable Church Multiplication Movements*. It's a breakthrough concept. It's a must read book.

~ **Luis Bush,**
International Facilitator,
Transform World Connections

Frank has provided what will prove to be an invaluable resource in the 21st century's unfolding of the Great Commission. He has included aspects that have largely been ignored, such as the importance of worldview and the combining of ecclesiology and anthropology with missiology. His "Wheel" is a very useful and comprehensive template to direct and guide. The questions in his concerns and criticisms certainly help us think, pray, and plan in a way to keep us on course. This book should be must reading for every missionary and mission student.

~ Gary Moore,
Lead Pastor, Hope Point Nazarene and
Field Strategy Coordinator, Northern Europe,
Church of the Nazarene

Do you aim to see churches multiply in the normal New Testament way? If so, you will find liberating insights in Frank Schattner's in-depth analysis of both historical progression and current movements. If your progress has slowed, then his comprehensive tables and practical summaries of effective strategies and guidelines will help you detect blind spots in your strategy.

~ George Patterson,
Founder *"Train & Multiply"*

the wheel model

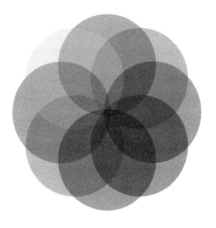

Catalyzing Sustainable Church
Multiplication Movements

Frank Schattner

Copyright ©2014
The Wheel Model: Catalyzing Sustainable Church Multiplication Movements/ Frank Schattner

www.hill111.com

ISBN 978-0-9916111-0-2

All rights reserved. Except for brief quotations in critical publications or reviews, no part of this book may be reproduced in any manner without prior written permission from the publisher.

www.jessup.edu

All references to Scripture have been taken from the HOLY BIBLE, NEW INTERNATIONAL VERSION®. Copyright © 1973, 1978, 1984 Biblica. Used by permission of Zondervan. All rights reserved.

The "NIV" and "New International Version" trademarks are registered in the United States Patent and Trademark Office by Biblica. Use of either trademark requires the permission of Biblica.

Cover and Interior Design: Dust Jacket Press Creative Art Department

Printed in United States of America

www.jessup.edu

DEDICATION

This book is dedicated to my three sons:
Ryan, Joshua and Nathan.

I learned many of the principles I write
about in this book while we lived in
Amber Creek village, North Thailand.
You boys are so precious to me;
you have brought so much joy to
your mother and me.

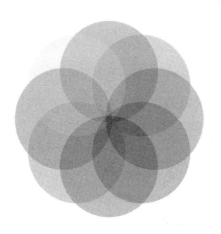

CONTENTS

Foreword xiii

Preface xv

Acknowledgments.. xvii

Abbreviations... xxi

CHAPTER 1: What's All This Chatter About CPMs? 1

CHAPTER 2: Meet the Past Players 13

CHAPTER 3: From CGM to CPMs 29

CHAPTER 4: A Fourth Era of Missions?........................ 51

CHAPTER 5: CPM Concerns & Criticisms 63

CHAPTER 6: The Wheel Model 85

CHAPTER 7: The Wheel Model vs. CPMs & the Critics 103

Definitions... 121

Notes 125

References 129

Appendix – Wheel Assessment Tool 135

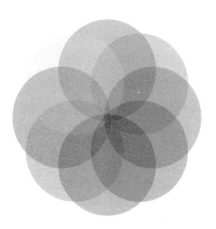

FOREWORD

Advancing the Kingdom of God is the purpose of all creation. It seems appropriate that this book presents a wheel model. The wheel has long been a symbol of advancement and progress.

Throughout history, every generation of saints stands on the shoulders of previous generations, striving for more fruit for the kingdom and more glory to God. In our generation, great progress has been made in fruitful ministry, especially among the "hard" people groups and in the "difficult" places. Frank Schattner's contribution to this progress is represented in this volume. His model helps to clarify and refine the advancements of our generation.

Frank is no ivory tower theoretician. Far from it. He is an old-school (in the best sense of the term) missionary. He is also a skeptical pragmatist (again in the best sense of the term). He has proven these principles in his own work, observed them in the multiple ministries of those whom he coaches, and verified them through discussion with coworkers. In this book he shares the distillation of his insights.

I urge you to learn from this work in the spirit in which it was written, not as a mere cookbook or checklist, but as a description of how God is working in the world. The intention of this volume is to encourage all God's people to listen attentively to the Spirit of God, discern his leadership in passionate persistent prayer, and respond through faithful service characterized by loving obedience and faithful stewardship of relationships, time, strengths, and resources.

This book is a tool and an encouragement to fulfill the Great Commission as quickly as possible, making disciples who are worth reproducing—disciples who display the faith of Jonathan for God's glory. As Jonathan said, "God is not limited to save, whether by many or by few" (1 Sam. 14:6). God responded to Jonathan's faith by providing a great victory against seemingly impossible odds. Wherever the Lord has called you to serve, I pray you will demonstrate similar faith and the Lord will also glorify himself through you in amazing ways.

To Hasten the Day,

Curtis Sergeant
January 22, 2014

PREFACE

The interest in Church Planting Movements (CPMs) as described by David Garrison in his two books, entitled the same, has generated considerable interest and discussion in the missions world. In these books Garrison presented anecdotal case studies describing unprecedented numbers of church plants within very short periods of time. He then summarized universal and common factors inherent within the CPMs.

As time progressed, however, criticisms began to emerge regarding the authenticity of some of the reported movements. These reports began to generate questions as to the authenticity and sustainability of CPMs. It was time to take an in-depth look at what was really happening out there. This book provides a biblical and historical backdrop for church multiplication and church movements while specifically exploring best practices that contribute to the sustainability of CPMs.

Until now, no one has conducted research in order to discover how experienced CPM practitioners define sustainability within a CPM, or the practices that sustains a CPM. For this book,[1] I interviewed twenty-three experienced CPM practitioners, a few of whom have seen movements of over a million people, asking them to identify specific fruitful practices that helped produce a sustained movement within their ministry context.

Eleven themes emerged from the study which I have grouped into three categories: (1) Core (Holy Spirit, Vision); (2) Fruitful Practices (Mission, Reproduction, Worldview Transformation, Ecclesiology, Leadership); and (3) Universals (Training, Modeling, Indigenization, Prayer). In the final chapter, I integrated the three categories into a visual model called the Wheel Model. This model provides the necessary framework for sustaining a church multiplication movement.

If CPM practitioners can successfully integrate the five fruitful practices simultaneously, a sustained movement should result in that it incorporates the best of what has been learned to date from both the Church Growth Movement (CGM) and the CPM. The principle-driven Wheel Model just may be the CPM model required for the Fourth Era of missions.

The back of the book contains an assessment tool to help track how well one is moving towards a Sustainable Church Multiplication Movement.

---

[1] *This book is an abridgement and adaptation of my dissertation entitled, Sustainability Within Church Planting Movements in East Asia, 2013.*

ACKNOWLEDGEMENTS

What a pleasure to write this book! In it I sought to add to the ongoing debate about how to practically apply Church Growth principles today. As followers of Christ who take the Great Commission seriously, every effort possible must be made to become better equipped as we co-mission with Christ. The unfinished task remains significant but also provides continued opportunities to witness firsthand God's eternal purpose to draw all peoples to himself. I sincerely hope and pray that this book will honor the contributions of past and present strategists and/or practitioners.

Writing this book was a significant challenge and I would be remiss if I failed to acknowledge those that have made noteworthy contributions. Dr. Tom Steffen, originally my doctoral advisor at Biola, has helped in numerous ways. His advisory role both during the writing of the dissertation and in editing this book has been invaluable. I am indebted and grateful for his role. Thanks Tom for being so tough; though you do it with such a winsome smile!

My international assistant for the Jonathan Project, Andy Smith of OMF, has also played a significant role. Thanks Andy for all the little things you do for me and the Jonathan Project ministry. I will be forever indebted to you.

OMF sponsored this research project. During the difficult moments of my studies and writing, I often gained strength knowing the unique privilege OMF made possible. I want to especially thank Sam Wunderlie, Sydney Witbooi, and Richard Schlitt for suggesting this research topic. Richard Schlitt, International Director of OMF, helped decide the research title. A big "thank you" to all my OMF friends! I will always feel indebted and grateful.

Mentors have played a very significant role in my life and I would like to highlight three. First, Bryce Jessup is my father-in-law and President Emeritus at William Jessup University. Thanks Bryce for being such a great role model not only to me but also to my three sons. Second, Jim Morris is an OMF pioneer missionary and visionary. Thanks Jim for your many years of encouragement and for passing on your legacy of faith to me. I will always feel indebted to you for many things, but especially for encouraging me to never quit! I would not still be in missions today if it were not for you. Finally, Neil Pomeroy, with the Navigators, mentored me for four years (1974–1978) while I was a student at the University of Massachusetts. My basic DNA to reproduce according to 2 Tim. 2:2 was formed under his leadership. Thanks Neil for spending so much time investing in me. I have tried to apply what you taught throughout my life.

As with all significant projects, family support is essential. My wife Jan and our three boys often had to put up with a distracted husband and father! Thank you sweetheart for being there and taking up the slack, especially while I was writing the dissertation. I know I could not have done this without your love and support.

Also while writing the book, I often reflected on my parents, Withold and Irene, who brought our family to the US after their respective families lost everything in Eastern Europe to the communists after the war. Coming to the US afforded me unique opportunities for which I have been very grateful. Thanks Opa and Oma!

Finally, and most importantly, I am grateful to my Savior, Lord, and King, Jesus Christ. He changed my life and moved me into directions I would have never imagined. It has been a great ride and I am so grateful. Thank you Lord for reaching down and touching a young teenager that was reaching up to find you. I have tried to make my life count in response to your wonderful grace!

Many other strategists and practitioners noted in the book have made significant contributions to sustainable church multiplication movements. Thank you to each and every one of you.

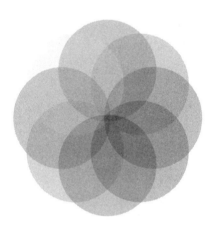

ABBREVIATIONS

AICS Academy of Integrated Christian Studies
CGM Church Growth Movement
CMM Church Multiplication Movement
COMIBAM COngreso Misionera IBeroAmericana
CPM Church Planting Movements
CSF Critical Success Factor
DAWN Discipling a Whole Nation
HUP Homogeneous Unit Principle
IBCM Indigenous Biblical Church Movements
IMB International Mission Board
JP Jonathan Project
JT Jonathan Training
KRA Key Result Area
MUP Mission to Unreached Peoples
OMF Overseas Missionary Fellowship
PM People Movement
SC Strategy Coordinator
S-CMM Sustainable Church Multiplication Movement
SEANet South, East, Southeast and North Asia Network
SWM School of World Missions
T4T Training for Trainers
UPG Unreached People Group
USCWM United States Center for World Mission
WRG Worldview Research Group

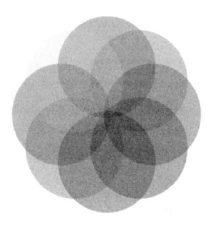

CHAPTER 1

WHAT'S ALL THIS CHATTER ABOUT CPMs?

Jesus said, "This gospel of the kingdom will be preached in the whole world as a testimony to all nations, then the end will come" (Matt. 24:14, NIV[1]). During the final decade of the 20th century, the A.D. 2000 Movement was born. Luis Bush led the new movement originating out of the Lausanne II international missions conference in Manila in 1989. This movement helped catalyze the global Church for the purpose of "establishing a church within every unreached people group [UPG] and making the gospel available to every person by the year 2000." Parallels to Matthew 24:14 become obvious.

As a result of the A.D. 2000 vision, some organizations, like the International Mission Board (IMB) of the Southern Baptist denomination, began to reevaluate their church planting models in light of this vision, and the fact that many unreached people groups (UPGs) resided within political boundaries closed to traditional, residential missionary approaches.

In the late 1980s, the IMB established a rapid advance team to explore new approaches to church planting in Asia that would result in the complete evangelization of UPGs. Some of these first pioneers included: David Watson, Bill Smith, Curtis Sergeant, and Bruce Carlton.

In the mid-1990s, reports began to emerge regarding unprecedented numbers of churches being planted. These pioneers eventually gathered into a forum for the express purpose of reflecting on "their shared experiences and then process them in a forum that invited critique and analysis."[2]

David Garrison's first book written in 1999, *Church Planting Movements,* documented the various phenomena occurring through the efforts of these pioneers. From the discussion Garrison identified 10 universal elements of a church planting movement (CPM). In addition, he defined a CPM as "a rapid and multiplicative increase of indigenous churches planting churches within a given people group or population segment."[3]

SOME BACKSTORY OF GOD AT WORK

Ying Kai, the son of a Taiwanese pastor, attended the IMB Strategy Coordinator (SC) training in 2000. Although trained as a traditional pastor, and typically starting two churches a year in Hong Kong as an IMB missionary, he prayerfully considered how the CPM principles he was learning could apply in a restrictive environment, such as China. Within three years, over 9,300 house churches/cells began. And the movement continues to explode. Training for Trainers (T4T) was born.[4]

Patrick Hobbs attended the Jonathan Training (JT) in Manila in 2001. As an experienced Overseas Missionary Fellowship (OMF) missionary he was committed to see Christ somehow transform the hopelessness found in the massive slums in Metro Manila. Prior to JT, holistic ministries undergirded by solid Bible teaching served as the main approach to meet the overwhelming physical and spiritual needs.

While at JT, Hobbs learned about the potential CPMs offered not only to plant multiplying churches, but also to socially transform people and societies. Hobbs prayerfully implemented a new strategy where church planting and multiplication were the leading edge, with an appropriate balance of social work. With this input, and ultimately the ownership of the local people, an evolving strategy was implemented. Within a few years, over 100 house churches/cells were started and lives were being transformed. Local people led all aspects of the church planting ministry with little, if any, outside financial help. Some of their best church planters were former drug dealers and prostitutes.[5]

In the early 1990s, Curtis Sergeant (who later became a key architect of Saddleback Church's PEACE Plan) attended Strategy Coordinator training as part of his required training as an IMB missionary. IMB assigned him and his young family to reach the Hainanese on the Chinese island province of Hainan located southeast of mainland China.

During the early stages of the ministry while riding on a bus, Sergeant witnessed as a grandmother with two young

The WHEEL MODEL

grandchildren crossing a street was hit by the bus in which he was riding. The grandmother was killed instantly. The bus driver continued driving saying, "That's her bad luck!"[6] The other passengers on the bus were too caught up in their own life struggles to even notice what happened. Sergeant prayerfully considered how to implement a CPM strategy on the island.

After witnessing the deep spiritual poverty of these people Sergeant was driven to his knees to develop a strategy that would expose the entire populace to the gospel. After many false starts, Sergeant settled on a simple church planting strategy for multiplying house churches. In a four-year period, believers went from 100 to 55,000, and the number of churches grew from three to over 500.[7] The work continues to expand without any further help from Sergeant.

The spiritual needs of a UPG, the Kaobu, were unanswered by the gospel until God raised up Taikadai and his family. Although cousins to the many Kaobu Christians in Thailand, significant language and cultural barriers exist, not to mention that the Kaobu live in the highly restrictive communist context of Laos. Roads and communication remain limited.

Taikadai took the Chiang Mai Jonathan Training in 2000 to learn about CPM methodology. In 2004, he gathered a team of locals and trained them in multiplication principles while emphasizing the authority of Scripture, removed extra-biblical requirements, and emphasized an oral approach among these illiterate people. Within six years a CPM took place with over 1,100 baptized believers. Ninety percent of the villages now have believers, and many have village house churches.

The Kaobu Church continues to expand while also reaching out to other unreached groups like the Thai Lue and Ahka. This all occurred under severe scrutiny and persecution.[8]

CRITICS BEGIN TO QUESTION CPMS

As Garrison's book gained notoriety, questions about CPMs began to arise. Many missionaries around the world questioned the anecdotal facts presented in the case studies in Garrison's book. Serious questions emerged when some of the case studies were found to be inaccurate, e.g., the Khmer of Cambodia.[9]

Some questioned the reports wondering what happened to the churches that were reportedly planted, while others queried if the number of reported planted churches had actually been planted. In other words, were the reports exaggerated? Were groups of believers that once gathered now defunct? The reported setbacks began to shine the light on the question of sustainability of the CPMs.

Tom Steffen, a critic of some aspects of CPMs, echoes the concerns of many in his book *The Facilitator Era: Beyond Pioneer Church Multiplication*:

> *One common value you will hear today is the desire for a sustainable movement. This value raises another question: sustainable in what areas? If sustainable refers to just keeping the movement going, I would have some deep reservations. Keeping a movement going that*

includes mostly those who have experienced deep worldview transformation is one thing. Keeping movements going without such transform-ation is a totally different matter.[10]

Ed Stetzer, a leading missiologist and former Director of Research for the North American Mission Board, generated a firestorm of interaction on a blog entitled "Monday is for Missiology: Second Thoughts on the Future of Missions." On February 28, 2011, Mark (no last name included), serving in Asia, highlighted the general reticence of many regarding Garrison's view of CPMs:

> *Dr. Sills cogently argues that CPM fails because it neglects training disciples and especially church leaders. Another weakness is that CPM has a weak ecclesiology. This has been pointed out by writers at 9Marks Ministries and Mid-America Seminary. Beyond that, many of the featured CPMs seem to have a short lifespan. That is, after a few years researchers cannot find the churches. In John 15:16, Jesus told his disciples 'I chose you and appointed you to bear fruit—fruit that will last.' It seems the rapidity emphasized by the CPM strategy does not produce fruit that lasts. I am not predicting that CPM will disappear overnight. Missions agencies change slowly; however, it does seem that CPM will slowly decline due to inherent weaknesses.*[11]

In his book *Reaching and Teaching: A Call to Great Commission Obedience,* David Sills emphasizes that "it is time for missionaries and missiologists to slow down their breakneck pace of ever-increasing speed and return to fulfilling the Great Commission to make disciples by teaching them to observe all that Jesus commanded us."[12]

> More recently, critique related to holism has emerged. Here again, Steffen is helpful as a leading voice for integrating the social and CPMs that produce an "authentic CPM":
>
> Part of an authentic CPM for me includes obedience to the Great Commandment. While this factor may slow down the rapidity of a movement, it says to all within hearing that Christianity is a total way of life that addresses all areas of life—the physical, emotional, intellectual, social, material, and spiritual—a message that really matters to those cultures that socialize their peoples to think holistically. Service ministries should accompany spiritual ministries. Even some BAM (Business as Mission) projects may be required. Transformational missiology should accompany frontier missiology.[13]

Steffen echoes the concerns of another critic, Bryant Myers, who advocates a more holistic approach to evangelism and church planting:

> *After all, God's story is about more than saving souls . . . the biblical account has a more holistic view of salvation, seeking the restoration by grace alone of our relationships with God, with each other, and with God's creation. While personal salvation through faith in Christ is the center of God's concern, it is not the limit of God's concern . . . God's concern for people as productive stewards living in just and peaceful relationships could emerge alongside God's concern for people living in right relationship with God.*[14]

In my experience working with local believers, mostly tribal, they also have doubts that echo some of the above concerns. Many have seen movements, large and small, among their own people. They understand that fellow tribal people are motivated to turn to Christianity for a host of reasons not necessarily related to the gospel, e.g., healings through power encounters. Similarly, Steffen reported another inherent weakness within a movement that occurred among the Palawanos in the Philippines in the mid-1950s, attributing a breakdown in the movement to a misunderstood gospel. The initial expatriate evangelist did not know how the gospel related to their culture.[15]

Among clan-based cultures, family ties create obligations that the Christian worker must consider. For example, a clan's local shaman may have converted, leaving the people with no spiritual leader to address a crisis, so they follow the shaman into Christianity.[16]

Clan farming obligations, as well as finding spouses for their children, can play a role in the conversion of large numbers. Additionally, receiving benefits from the missionary or mission, like hostels and schooling for their children, has also played a vital role. For example, a World Concern in-house report, *Khmer Leadership: Ancient Leadership and Current Practices* notes,

> Going to church or Christian outreach is for many an act of positioning oneself around a resource base or else around those who have access to that resource base. Social concern for saving face will motivate people to do and say whatever is necessary to fit in and show themselves agreeable to the church planter's purposes.[17]

This raises further questions. How solid is the gospel presentation? How is the gospel understood and proclaimed by locals? Has the metanarrative been captured?

Echoing the concerns of Steffen,[18] numerous local leaders that have experienced rapid growth of new believers and churches that I know do not seem that excited about CPMs. This rings especially true when they find themselves in the middle of a pastoral nightmare resulting from a poorly discipled movement that resulted in little or no worldview transformation.

Steffen highlights worldview transformation in a case study from a South American ministry entitled "Ibero-

American COMIBAM International (COngreso Misionera IBero Americana) and the Role of Worldview Resource Group (WRG)" in this ministry. "WRG believes that the degree to which the worldview of the host society is brought into tension and is transformed by a biblical worldview is the degree to which the church plant will be successful."[19]

Some critics have theological concerns. The JT provides basic CPM training mainly for those serving among UPGs. A primary concern often emerging among the attendees is whether or not CPMs have biblical precedence. Taking the trainees through portions of the book of Acts where movements are described often dispels such doubts. For example, during a recent JT in Taiwan, the coordinator of the training reported that,

> *The 90 minutes of Acts study each morning was key. It did most of the work for us – all the convincing ... It also kept the whole question focused on "Where do you get that idea - i.e. what does the Book say?" This sorted out many traditionalists.*[20]

Craig Ott and Gene Wilson highlight their central concern with Garrison's description of CPMs in their book *Global Church Planting*: "Unlike Garrison, we are concerned less with a rapid multiplication than with healthy multiplication."[21]

The above comments and questions highlight the need to address the concerns and criticisms of the critics summarized under one thematic heading—sustainability.

During a visit in August 2010 with J. D. Payne, former Director of Church Planting at the Southern Baptist Seminary in Louisville, Kentucky, he noted that no one has raised the specific question of sustainability in the context of church multiplication. He added that although this may be the current case, he sensed it will be a key question within the next five years.[22]

All the voices of concern related above echo the voice of Melvin Hodges' axiom: "The measure of true success is not that which the missionary accomplishes while on the field, but the work that still stands after he is gone."[23] Do CPMs remain sustainable?

SUMMARY

Despite various concerns and criticisms, interest in CPMs as described and documented by Garrison has spread like wildfire among the church planting missionary community. And there continues to be high interest in applying CPM principles in various contexts around the globe.

Even so, practitioners of CPM methodology, and critics alike, have raised a serious question that demands attention: Do CPMs remain sustainable? This book attempts to answer that question, as well as other related missiological questions.

I begin by reviewing some of the more influential players of the past.

The WHEEL MODEL

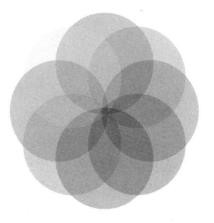

CHAPTER 2
MEET the PAST PLAYERS

The rapid growth of the church plays a key role in bringing closure to the Great Commission. The book of Acts demonstrates God's glory when large numbers of people entered the Church in a short period of time (Acts 2:41, 47; 4:4; 5:14; 6:1, 7; 9:31; 19:8-10; 26; 28:30-31).

With that said, missionaries over the centuries have generally resisted rapid growth methodologies and strategies because of the legitimate fear that such growth is often associated with the lack of spiritual depth. Christianity has far too often been defined as a mile wide and an inch deep. Even so, both qualitative growth and quantitative growth should happen simultaneously, whether growth is rapid or slow.

The concept of church planting movements has evolved over the centuries. In this chapter I will take a historical look at the growth of the church beginning with the New Testament. Then I will take a deeper look at how Church Growth theory began and evolved over time, focusing on the modern era of missions. William Carey, the father of modern missions, launched the Protestant missions movement in the early 1800s (First Era of modern missions, early 1800s). Since that initial launch, missionary practitioners began learning many missiological insights directly from the contexts in which they worked. The historical review will also examine the evolution of terms used to describe movements, its theology, and contributions gained over the Second (1865-1880), and Third Eras (1935-2000) of modern missions.

History reveals that these great servants of God have contributed significantly to present-day church movements through key principles that help present practitioners to better understand what sparks and sustains movements. I begin by laying a brief biblical and historical foundation, then quickly fast forward to the Protestant modern missions, taking a close look at some of the key players who participated in the second and third eras of modern missions.

BIBLICAL ACCOUNTS

While the New Testament never explicitly mentions the terms People Movements (PMs), Church Planting Movements (CPMs), or Indigenous Biblical Church Movements (IBCMs), it certainly supports a multiplication theology. The iconic verse that promotes multiplication originates from Jesus himself: "But the one who received the seed that fell on good soil is the man who hears the word and understands it. He produces a crop, yielding a hundred, sixty or thirty times what was sown" (Matt. 13:23).

Paul also stressed the centrality of multiplication in his church planting strategy when he wrote to his young protégé Timothy, "And the things you have heard me say in the presence of many witnesses entrust to reliable men who will also be qualified to teach others" (2 Tim. 2:2). Paul continues to echo his missional passion in his second letter to the Thessalonians: "...pray for us that the message of the Lord may spread rapidly and be honored just as it was with you" (2 Thess. 3:1).

Historians like Adolf Harnack would argue that the DNA for church multiplication was deeply rooted in the fertile soil of Paul's Judaism. Through Judaism, God cultivated the soil so evangelism and movements became part of the social fabric of the early church.[1]

Donald McGavran, a noted missiologist and father of the modern-day Church Growth movement, emphasized that "church growth is 'rooted' in theology. God wants church growth. He wants His lost children found. The multiplication of churches is theologically required."[2] Alan Tippett argued the same in *Church Growth and the Word of God*.

EARLY CHURCH/MISSIONARY HISTORY

Interest in facilitating Christ-ward movements among the unreached that results in the rapid planting of churches is certainly not new. Early missionaries in Europe, Patrick and Boniface thought strategically about what is now called CPMs.

Patrick of Ireland (AD 387-461)

Richard Fletcher's historical account of the conversion of Western Europe (4th - 14th centuries) details the life, ministry, and missionary strategies of Patrick. He writes that Patrick prayed for a movement among the European tribes.

> It was our bounden duty to spread our nets, so that a vast multitude and throng might be caught for God and there might be clergy everywhere to baptize and exhort a people that was poor and needy, as the Lord says; He urges and teaches in the gospel saying, "Go now, teach all nations."[3]

According to Fletcher, Patrick's approach was groundbreaking for his time:

> No one within Western Christendom had thought thoughts as these before, had ever been previously possessed by such convictions. As far as evidence goes, he was the first person in Christian history to take the scriptural injunctions literally; to grasp that teaching all nations meant teaching even the barbarians who lived beyond the frontiers of the Roman Empire.[4]

Because of such convictions embedded within the DNA of the Irish church, a high commitment to fulfilling the Great

Commission existed. Movements were an accepted element for fulfilling their missional responsibilities.

Patrick's missiological methods illustrate the first true example of whole people groups coming to Christ post-New Testament. Generations of missionaries would build upon these principles.

> **SIDEBAR 2.1**
> ***PATRICK'S MISSIOLOGICAL PRINCIPLES & PRACTICES***
> 1. Prayer produces movements.
> 2. Take the Bible's injunctions to reach the nations literally.
> 3. Movements fulfill missional responsibilities.

BONIFACE OR WYNFRITH OF CREDITON (AD 675-754)

Boniface, an Anglo-Saxon missionary, built on the successes of the Irish mission. By A.D. 750 he noticed that all the German tribes had been converted. Historical documents state that by A.D. 739 there were 100,000 German converts. However, conversions were very nominal. In light of the situation, Boniface introduced monasteries to provide the necessary training.[5]

Boniface challenged the worldview assumptions of the German people and engaged in power encounters, demonstrating that the God of Christianity was superior to all the German gods. One iconic story tells of Boniface chopping down the sacred oak of Thor at Geismar in Hesse and then using the wood to build a chapel.[6] Although a large number of Germans responded to Boniface's challenge in what would today be called a CPM, conversions again lacked spiritual depth.

Taking ecclesiology seriously, Boniface challenged the widespread nominalism endemic to the German Church (see: Sidebar 2.2). In spite of the nominalism, Christianity had a profound effect on the various people groups of northern Europe to the point where traditional tensions between people groups were completely pacified, adding even more appeal to the Christian faith.[7]

SIDEBAR 2.2
BONIFACE'S MISSIOLOGICAL PRINCIPLES & PRACTICES
1. New churches should be run well and be highly organized.
2. Baptize believers quickly and then teach them.
3. Value church discipline.
4. Practice cultural substitutes when supplanting pagan festivals.
5. Contextualize where possible.
6. Indigenize by preserving local languages instead of using Latin.[8]

MODERN ERA PLAYERS

Before William Carey (1761-1834), missions in the Protestant church was virtually nonexistent. The Catholic Church took the missionary mandate far more seriously than did the Protestants. William Carey changed all that.

Who helped develop the theories that would be used to fulfill the Great Commission and the Great Commandment during those early missions eras? I will now introduce some of the pioneers, beginning with John Nevius.

John Nevius (1829-1893)

Appointed by the American Presbyterian Mission, John Nevius served as a Protestant missionary in China and Korea. His classic, *The Planting & Development of Missionary Churches,* broke new ground. The principles and practices Nevius outlined continue into the 21st century.

Nevius began his missionary career in China where he was highly critical of the missionary efforts of his day. As a pragmatist, he believed the present practices produced dependency. So he began to implement unconventional principles and practices only to have his fellow missionaries reject them flatly. One colleague even wrote a book castigating his ideas. As a result, he was widely repudiated not only by the missionary community, but by the Chinese Christians as well.

Much of the criticism centered around Nevius' resistance to pay local workers to conduct ministry. He observed that paying local workers "sorely handicapped" them even if the philanthropy was born out of goodwill. Although not opposed to outside assistance, his resistance had to do with the question of how much support to allow.

Nevius recognized that his and other missionaries' goals were generally consistent. His objection had to do with *how* to achieve those goals as he was an ardent proponent of the indigenous principle of self-support.[9]

A key strategy Nevius employed to encourage indigenization during the second era of missions was the missionaries' role in training the Chinese to be trainers of other Chinese trainers. This would ensure the natural expansion of the Church through "godly lives and voluntary activities of its members."[10] This stood in stark contrast to paying locals to start new outstations, many of which were much weaker than those that were started without funding.[11]

Quoting a colleague, Nevius points out the severe negative effects of providing salaries for local workers:

> *We affirm without fear of contradiction, that no one thing has more effectively hindered the development of independent, self-sustaining native churches in many foreign fields than the high salaries which, with mistaken wisdom, are paid to many native pastors and helpers from the treasuries of the home church.*[12]

While Nevius's methods focused on church planting and the complete evangelization of a specific people group, he also warned about unhealthy motivations. "If the desire for tangible results should take the form of a wish to gather into the Church as soon as possible the greatest number of professed converts it may become a dangerous temptation and snare."[13]

Nevius faced great resistance within China where

traditional missions methods were deeply entrenched over many years of ministry. That would change dramatically when a new mission field would open.

In 1890, seven newly arrived missionaries in Korea invited Nevius to teach them the "Nevius Plan," which he did over a two-week period. The pioneers then vigorously applied the principles, and the rest is history. Testimonials directly attribute their success to the training that they believed was deeply grounded in the character of God, therefore, "the results were God's."[14]

A deeply spiritual man, Nevius based his principles on the practicality of God's Word, not on the expediency of the missionary context. See Sidebar 2.3 for other principles that drove Nevius' ministry.

> **SIDEBAR 2.3**
> **JOHN NEVIUS' MISSIOLOGICAL PRINCIPLES & PRACTICES**
>
> 1. Oral Bible stories.
> 2. Emphasize 2 Timothy 2:2 and obedience-based training.
> 3. Everyone is a learner and a teacher.
> 4. Expect locals, once trained, to multiply.
> 5. Give advanced training to only the best trainers.
> 6. Encourage locals to follow New Testament practices rather than Western models.
> 7. Rely on the Holy Spirit to provide life transformation with use of spiritual gifts for the growth and sanctification of the Church.

Gustav Warneck (1834-1910)

A German missionary with the Rheinish Mission to the Battaks of Sumatra, Gustav Warneck, pioneered missionary principles and practices a century ahead of their time. He was a brilliant thinker, strategist, and theologian, not to mention a prolific writer. Sadly, many of his writings were buried in history due to Germany's role in two world wars.

His monumental book, *The Living Christ and Dying Heathenism (1954)*, is considered one of the finest explanations of animism and how worldview transformation results through the power of the gospel. He believed that elements of the gospel itself had divine power to break the strongholds of animism and unbelief. God had placed a God vacuum in each person's consciousness, which he compared to iron. That consciousness, when confronted with the magnet-like gospel, acts as a force to draw out the truth that enables the "heathen" to comprehend the truth of the gospel.[15]

In order to present the saving message of Christ to the "heathen," he relied on narrated stories from the Old and New Testaments. "A new religious world is dawning upon the heathen through the simple narration of what God has done."[16]

The burning question that drove his ministry was, "Are vital powers imported into and become operative in the heathen world through the preaching of the gospel; what are those quickening gospel powers?"[17] Warneck believed the driving force that changed the inertia of unbelief within a people group was the gospel itself, typified in the Old Testament, and ultimately revealed in the living Christ.

Warneck influenced many missionaries, the most noteworthy at the time being Christian Keysser. Regarding the complete evangelization of a people group, Keysser quoted Warneck as saying, "People Movements are essential to reach the 'individual.'"[18]

SIDEBAR 2.4
G. WARNECK'S MISSIOLOGICAL PRINCIPLES & PRACTICES

1. The gospel has the innate power to break animism.
2. Reaching individuals requires group movements.

Christian Keysser (1877-1961)

In the forward of *A People Reborn*, McGavran praised Christian Keysser as a preeminent missiologist even before the term was coined.[19] A man ahead of his time, Keysser shaped missionary practice that would affect future generations.

Although a proponent of movements among his host people, the Papuans, Keysser's focused on the transformation of a people group, and the complete indigenization of the gospel among them. As McGavran notes,

> *He [was] not concerned whether few or many are baptized. He [was] concerned that the life of Christ be reproduced in the New Guinea congregation....He believed that*

> *these people [were] abundantly able to be good Christians within their tribal context, while being thoroughly themselves.*[20]

In other words, in order to sustain a movement among a people group, transformation and indigenization were two key factors for Keysser. A movement was simply the catalyst in that transformation process.

Keysser also emphasized ecclesiology and often berated German theologians for offering up theologies that had little if anything to do with the life of the Church. "Because we in the homeland only look after theology and doctrine and not God's reality and power at work, we have the present lamentable weakness of the church. Deadness is prevalent despite all good doctrine."[21]

As a student of Warneck, Keysser became a keen observer of tribal culture. Early in his ministry he realized that the social organization and values of tribal people were entirely different from those of Europeans. Initially when Papuans wanted to convert as a group, he resisted and stood in their way. Ultimately, he titled his futile efforts as a "clear fiasco."[22]

Being a deeply practical and spiritual man, he finally realized that God was fine with saving the people as a whole group. He realized missions history confirmed PMs, noting that his own people, the Germans, converted through a PM. He ultimately concluded that, "Tribes will convert as a group no matter what the missionary thinks or wants."[23] See Sidebar 2.5 for other principles and practices of Keysser, many of which are imbedded in current CPMs.

> **SIDEBAR 2.5**
> **C. KEYSSER'S MISSIOLOGICAL PRINCIPLES & PRACTICES**
>
> 1. Lay a foundation for the gospel from the Old Testament.
> 2. Use Bible stories.
> 3. Teach literacy to all converts.
> 4. Stress indigenization in all aspects of the ministry to help assure sustainability.
> 5. Aim for a people movement that includes the whole tribe because "defection from the tribe was considered immoral, irresponsible and even unnatural."[24]
> 6. Stress contextualization in all aspects of the work to enhance conversion of the whole tribe.
> 7. Aim for worldview transformation that leads to societal transformation.
> 8. Emphasize obedience to God's Word.
> 9. Missionaries should plan both their entry and exit strategies.

Keysser, a major player during the third era of missions, challenged many of the colonial attitudes and missionary practices of his day. For that, he was often repudiated and his principles ignored. Time, however, has validated the wisdom of his missiological practices.

Roland Allen (1868-1947)

Roland Allen, an English missionary, spent a few years in northern China as a member of The Society for the Propagation of the Gospel. Ultimately, he finished his missionary career in Kenya which was cut short because of health problems.[25]

The missionary centric and paternalistic way they

conducted church planting disillusioned Allen. After some reflection and becoming familiar with Rufus Anderson and Henry Venn's Three-Self theory (self-governing, self-supporting, self- propagating), he penned a number of books that challenged the status quo of missionary practices in his era. His most noteworthy books include *The Spontaneous Expansion of the Church*, *Missionary Methods: St. Paul's or Ours*, and *Missionary Principles*. Even though he wrote in the 1920s, his books remain instructive today.

Reading Allen's books is a must for any serious missionary student, even if he appears haughty at times, seeming to elevate himself as an armchair missiologist while criticizing missionary practitioners. Even so, he correctly argued that mission-planted churches should be self-propagating, self-governing, and self-supporting from their inception. He defined spontaneous expansion as

The unexhorted and unorganized activity of individual members of the church, explaining to others the gospel which they have found for themselves; the expansion which follows the irresistible attraction of the Christian Church for men who see its ordered life, and are drawn to it by desire to discover the secret of life which they instinctively desire to share; and the expansion of Church by the addition of new churches.[26]

Never one to avoid the hard questions, Allen challenged the mission executives of his day, asking a question that remains relevant today, "Are we actually planting new churches or merely perpetuating a mission."[27]

While Allen proposed many principles that were grounded in Pauline theology and solid missiology, he still held a traditional church model that was typically Western in ecclesiology and structure. He preferred buildings for churches. See Sidebar 2.6 for other Allen contributions.

SIDEBAR 2.6
R. ALLEN'S MISSIOLOGICAL PRINCIPLES & PRACTICES

1. Emphasize the role of the Holy Spirit in church planting.
2. Indigenize right from the beginning.
3. Stress that the multiplication of Christians must be accompanied by the multiplication of churches.
4. Recognize that multiplication and discipleship can go hand-in-hand.
5. Focus on conversion first, then social programs.
6. Acknowledge that the methods used really do matter.

SUMMARY

These great minds were products of the first and second eras of modern missions, some of which were influenced by the Student Volunteer Movement founded in 1886. They unleashed huge intellectual potential for mission service. As a result, profound missiological thinking became crystallized through the Church Growth Movement, providing the foundational underpinnings for 21st century missiological practice.

I will now consider how the Church Growth Movement influenced CPMs.

The WHEEL MODEL

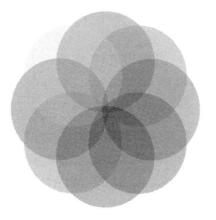

CHAPTER 3

FROM CGM to CPMs

The 1930s launched the Third Era of the modern missionary movement. Names like Cameron Townsend and Donald McGavran loom large during this era. The seed thoughts of PMs sown in the Second Era would crystallize during the Third Era. Even more importantly, they would challenge missionary efforts to move beyond conducting helpful ministries on the mission field to making church growth a key result area (KRA).

In this chapter I will note the influence that the Church Growth Movement (CGM) has had on CPMs. David Garrison's role in advocating CPMs follows. I begin with J. W. Pickett who would light a fire under Donald McGavran, a premier missiologist in the Third Era, who became known as the father of the modern-day CGM.

J. Waskom Pickett (1890-1981)

J. Waskom Pickett, an American missionary with the Methodist Church, had a long and illustrious career among various castes in India. He was a child prodigy, and like all great missiologists before and after he had a great mind, maybe the greatest. The average student may find his writings weighty and difficult to comprehend.[1]

A man of passion for the things of God and a keen observer of missiological insights, Pickett noted the societal factors that enhanced the complete evangelization of a people group. *Christian Mass Movements in India,* a book that Donald McGavran later called "epochal,"[2] captured his initial thinking. Picket emphasized that communal cultures naturally respond to the gospel as a whole group. This concept flew in the face of individual conversions, a concept natural to missionaries coming from Western societies.

Pickett used the term "extraction" to describe the typical approach to evangelism and church planting practiced by missionaries of his day. Missionaries would target individuals irrespective of their social networks, convert them, and then incorporate them into a church made up of a mixture of tribes or castes. Since there was no social or familial connection between members of the congregations, creating a sense of community became difficult. Even more critical, it cut off relationships with family members.

Pickett's proposal to have groups convert collectively was imminently more productive and consistent with Scripture, making the complete evangelization of a people group possible. See Sidebar 3.1 for other missiological principles Pickett promoted.

After retiring from 46 years of outstanding missionary service in India, Pickett continued to encourage McGavran to promote church growth principles primarily through the School of Church Growth at Fuller Theological Seminary in Pasadena, California. Although never a faculty member, Pickett delivered the annual Church Growth lecture in 1961.[3]

SIDEBAR 3.1
J. WASKOM PICKETT'S MISSIOLOGICAL PRINCIPLES & PRACTICES

1. Rapid church growth produces healthier churches.
2. Slow growth attitude is sin, reflecting complacency.
3. Social ministries should always be connected to church planting, but secondary.
4. Partnerships of missionaries and locals typically produced growth.
5. Faith is key to effective church growth.

Donald McGavran (1897-1990)

Born in India to missionary parents, Donald McGavran later returned to India as a missionary with the Disciples of Christ for 33 years. While in India, Pickett had significant influence on McGavran.

> *While God has granted me a part in the process, I neither invented church growth nor am solely responsible for it. Indeed, I owe my interest in church growth to a great Methodist*

> bishop, Jarrell Waskom Pickett. In 1934, he kindled my concern that the Church grow. I lit my candle at his fire.[4]

Popularly known as the father of the CGM, McGavran immeasurably influenced church planters, missionaries, and missiologists around the world. Part of his appeal included his enthusiastic demeanor. Arthur Glasser, a colleague at Fuller's School of World Missions (SWM), noted, "McGavran is an enthusiast, a 'vibrator' in the best sense of the word. He can convey a glow. He has the thrust to his personality that would qualify him as a leader."[5]

Greg Parsons pointed out that when McGavran first became acquainted with Pickett's work, he had serious doubts about reports of large numbers of people coming to Christ in groups.[6] After working and studying with Pickett for 20 years, McGavran became convinced about the church growth principles Pickett advocated.

This understanding resulted in McGavran's first groundbreaking book entitled *The Bridges of God*. Vernon Middleton, a personal friend and student of McGavran, argued that the book became the "most read missionary book in 1956."[7]

McGavran's influence continued to extend through many other key books and writings, most notably, *How Churches Grow, Church Growth and Group Conversion, Crucial Issues in Missions Tomorrow (1972), Momentous Decisions in Missions Today,* and his *magnum opus* in 1970, *Understanding Church Growth*.

The ideas Pickett advocated spread globally among the missionary world because of McGavran's influence. Arthur McPhee credits McGavran with popularizing Pickett's church growth principles.

> Had he [McGavran] not realized the value of Pickett's insights, and had he not tirelessly worked on, discovered their international relevance, and had he not tirelessly worked at refining and communicating the concepts until the missiological world could no longer ignore them, Pickett's powerful ideas would probably have died in 1930's India.[8]

One of those principles that McGavran advocated pertained to people movements. Echoing Pickett, McGavran argued, "Christward movements of people are the supreme goal of missionary effort."[9]

McGavran's influential thinking extended through the Institute of Church Growth, established in 1961 in Eugene, Oregon. Glasser, who succeeded McGavran as Dean of the School of World Missions (SWM), believed this was the actual beginning of the CGM. "In my judgment the church growth movement actually began in January, 1961, when McGavran founded what he called the *Institute Of Church Growth* in an unused corner of the library of a small Christian college (currently Northwest Christian University) in remote Eugene, Oregon."[10] In 1965, he moved the training center to the campus of Fuller Theological Seminary in Pasadena, California, where he founded the School of World Missions.

The single idea that represents the seed thought of the CGM is simply this: people groups will convert more readily, more rapidly, and in larger numbers when they convert as a whole people group, thus enabling them to maintain all their social networks. In other words, McGavran stressed a sociological principle, applying it to missionary evangelism and church planting: "People like to become Christians without crossing racial, linguistic or class barriers."[11]

Donald Wodarz, a priest in the Society of Saint Columban, summarized what he believed to be the essence of McGavran's Church Growth principles taken from his seminal book, *Understanding Church Growth:*

> *Churches grow in those places where Christians involve themselves in seeking and finding the lost sheep, bringing them into the master's fold, and feeding, pasturing those brought into the fold. Faithfulness in proclamation, calling to repentance, or finding the lost is not enough; those who have heard, who have repented must be brought into congregations, they must be taken into folds where they are nourished and fed with the Word of God.*[12]

A concept that remains at the very core of the CGM is the Homogeneous Unit Principle (HUP). The HUP is based on "the idea that people are made up of distinct groupings or homogeneous units of peoples or people groups. If the gospel makes sense in terms of their cultural context, people tend to come to Christ in larger numbers."[13]

McGavran, as well as others in the CGM, never advocated that a movement was an end in itself, but was simply a necessary preliminary means toward the complete evangelization of a people group.[14] As a result of his research, McGavran argued that two-thirds of Christianized people today came to Christ through a PM.[15]

Beyond the seminal PMs concept, much of McGavran's church planting methodology still did not discourage the construction of traditional Western church buildings or Western ecclesiology, and he was not opposed to paying local workers,[16] two principles inconsistent with CPM principles. However, his most comprehensive work, *Understanding Church Growth (1970)*, promotes the multiplication of churches in homes and the gathering of new believers into cell groups.[17] See Sidebar 3.2 for other McGavran missiological contributions.

SIDEBAR 3.2
D. MCGAVRAN'S MISSIOLOGICAL PRINCIPLES & PRACTICES

1. Replaced "mass movement" with "people movement."
2. Social ministries take second place to evangelism.
3. Challenged the prevailing ideology/theology that slow growth equals good missions.
4. The gospel is central and even takes precedence over a PM.
5. Train missionaries and locals in church multiplication principles.
6. Allocate limited resources to the most responsive peoples.

7. Ministry research should be priority and funded.
8. Church growth goals should be measured to assure success.
9. Missionaries should not remain long among a people group.

Alan Tippett (1911-1988)

A historian/anthropologist/missionary, Australian Alan Tippett served in the Fiji islands for over 20 years under the Methodists. Tippett later joined the faculty at Fuller's School of World Missions where he taught missionary anthropology, a discipline still in its infancy at that time.

Like other missiologists of his era, Tippett was a keen observer of how people groups converted, having witnessed this firsthand in Fiji. His field experience and training made it possible to contribute to Church Growth theory by adding anthropological and theological insights: "Church Growth is anthropologically, indigenously and biblically based."[18] He emphasized that there should be balance between theology and anthropology, otherwise church growth would be obstructed.

One of Tippett's key contributions to the CGM was his understanding and description of how animists convert to Christ. Power encounter stood at the center of the conversion process, a concept he argued that was woefully neglected in Western seminaries: "When that evangelist is trained in Western seminary, Bultmann and Hoekendijk have not given him or her much equipment to deal with it [power encounter] for the Lord."[19]

In *Verdict Theology,* Tippett details the conversion process of animists. The role of the missionary in this process is to direct change from the old context of paganism toward the new context of Christianity. Tippett describes the process:

> Conversion as a process begins with a certain awareness. The meaning of the Gospel as advocated may be not clear but some awareness of an option is there. At the point of realization it suddenly becomes relevant. It becomes recognizable as an option for the group (or individual). Then follows the period of decision-making, which, like the period awareness, may be short or long. In the case of group decision, which is multi-individual, it may involve long discussions spread over a year or more. Ultimately they are brought to the point of encounter, which in Oceania will be manifest in some act like fetish-burning. Finally there needs to be some act of incorporation whereby the decision-making is consummated by bringing the group in the Christian community so they know who they are and where they belong in the new context.[20]

Figure 1 illustrates Tippett's schematic of the conversion process.

The WHEEL MODEL

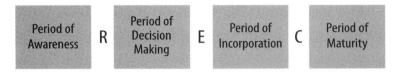

R = Point of Realization, E = Point of Encounter, C = Point of Consummation

Like his predecessors, Tippett believed that ultimately church growth is the divine work of God. He also argued that God had delegated people a specific role in the process.[22] Tippet also agreed with his contemporaries that church growth was not an end in itself. In this area he preferred to follow McGavran by promoting "perfection growth."[23]

In Tippett's mind, mere Christian presence promoted an inadequate description of Christianity. Church growth, quantitatively as well as qualitatively, must become the key measures of success. He insisted that methods should always be reevaluated in terms of results. "The missionary strategists who nonchalantly rejects church growth as an adequate approach to mission are usually conditioned by a theology of pessimism."[24]

Ralph Winter (1924-2009)

An American missiologist and Presbyterian missionary with an engineering background, Ralph Winter ministered among the Mayan Indians of Guatemala. While in Guatemala, he and others implemented Theological Education by Extension (TEE) that eventually became popular globally.

In 1974, as a plenary speaker at the Congress for World Evangelization in Lausanne, Switzerland, Winter intentionally unsettled the missionary community by highlighting the need to focus on the unengaged UPGs around the world.[25] He argued that if there was any hope in bringing closure to the Great Commission then the most strategic task of missions was to engage in Evangelism 2 (E2) [near cultures] and Evangelism 3 (E3) [distant cultures].

Today, E2 and E3 would be identified as Church Planting 2 (CP2) and Church Planting 3 (CP3), i.e., planting churches cross-culturally within near cultures or distant cultures. Many consider Winter's emphasis on E2 and E3 during his 1974 presentation as a watershed moment for global missions.

To continue to raise awareness about UPGs, and after teaching missions history at Fuller SWM, Winter founded the U.S. Center for World Mission (USCWM) in Pasadena, California. Charles Kraft, a colleague at the SWM, describes Winter as the most interesting and "one of the most innovative missiological thinkers of the twentieth century."[26]

A brilliant missiologist, Winter mobilized the global church through other programs like the *Perspectives on the World Christian Movement* course, as well as William Carey International University, and the International Society for Frontier Missiology. The William Carey bookstore is also located on the USCWM campus. Kraft believes that of all Winter's innovative achievements during his career, the Perspectives course may be his signature accomplishment.[27]

While Winter did not add to McGavran's ideas on PMs, or the homogeneous unit principle, his major contribution centered on his sharp focus to identify, categorize, strategize, and engage UPGs around the world. Winter's nuanced emphasis on "hidden people" and "UPGs" would become a key tactical missiological focus for bringing closure to the Great Commission.

People like C. P. Wagner, for example, focused on existing local churches, helping them to increase in size and grow spiritually. Winter, on the other hand, focused on areas where the churched did not yet exist.[28] That focus acted as a catalyst to CPMs among the least reached peoples around the world.

C. Peter Wagner (1930-)

C. Peter Wagner was born in the Big Apple, New York City, into a non-Christian family. As a young man he enrolled in the College of Agriculture at Rutgers University, preparing for a career in dairy farming. While there, he distinguished himself as a drunkard and profaner.[29]

When he met the love of his life, Doris, a devoted Christian, she led him to Christ. Wagner then attended Fuller Theological Seminary, graduating in 1955. Shortly after, he and Doris joined the South American Indian Mission and moved to Bolivia.

After their first term they transferred to the Bolivian Indian Mission (now Serving In Mission). While in Bolivia, Wagner read McGavran's *Bridges of God,* and was not initially impressed. In 1966, he decided to return to Fuller to study under McGavran in the SWM.

An enthusiastic and engaging student, he soon caught the eye of McGavran who eventually invited him to join the SWM faculty. An avid disciple of McGavran's Church Growth theories, Wagner became McGavran's understudy at SWM. While there, he began to consider how Church Growth principles would work in the United States. As he began teaching American pastors, the CGM in the United States began to move in a direction that McGavran never intended, growing churches bigger and better rather than multiplying them.

Kraft describes Wagner's influence on American churches as the "enthusiastic reception and application of Church Growth theory by American pastors and churches has provided an energy on the American church scene probably not experienced since the Awakenings of the seventeenth and eighteenth centuries."[30]

In 1980, Kraft had another epiphany, "It had become clear to me that there must have been a concomitant spiritual dimension to Church Growth that Donald McGavran had not particularly emphasized in his teaching and writing."[31] From that point on, he, along with the late John Wimber, began to teach about the power dimension of the Great Commission. Wagner soon joined in as well, challenging the status quo of missions in relation to the use of signs and wonders and spiritual warfare.[32]

CHURCH PLANTING MOVEMENTS

The CPM has moved beyond the CGM. The context in which Christian workers conduct missions today has changed drastically, and consequently, so have the ministry models and strategies. That is because each modern missions era faced a different geopolitical landscape. Does the emergence of the CPM serve as a harbinger indicating that a new era of missions has arrived? Has a Fourth Era replaced the Third Era?

Pioneers of the CGM were keen observers of how people groups converted to Christ. David Garrison and his colleagues continued the reflection, identifying universal elements (which focused strongly on how churches multiply) inherent within any church movement. Garrison ultimately coined the phrase "Church Planting Movement," or more popularly, "CPM."[33]

David Garrison (1958-)

An American missionary researcher with the International Mission Board (IMB) of the Southern Baptists, David Garrison evaluates church planting from a missiological perspective by observing praxis on the field. He gathers firsthand anecdotal evidence from experienced practitioners, compiles it, and evaluates it for the purposes of understanding CPMs.

Garrison has planted churches in India and coached other CPM practitioners in several countries while continuing to be a keen observer of experienced practitioners around the world. Having lived in seven countries, traveled to 80 others, and studied a dozen languages, he continues to be both a student and practitioner of CPMs worldwide.[34] Garrison follows the tradition of other leading missiologists who have a passion for God and a great ability to communicate what God seems to be teaching the missions community.

Garrison's Influence

Garrison's two books, *Church Planting Movements* published in 1999 and 2004, have sent shockwaves throughout the mission world, similar to what McGavran's *The Bridges of God* did in 1955. He describes what God seems to be doing through CPMs as a key process in the complete evangelization of a people group.

His approach is descriptive and anecdotal, his books instructive, having a prophetic ring. *Church Planting Movements* and some 20 articles describe certain universals inherent in every CPM along with critical factors. Garrison challenges church planters to avoid obstacles that can hinder God's working in bringing about a movement. Although his books are groundbreaking in many ways, careful observation discloses that the roots of Garrison's 10 universals and critical factors find their DNA in McGavran's writings.

CGM AND CPM DISTINCTIONS

Does the CPM have distinguishing characteristics that differ from those of the CGM? Garrison believes so, noting the following: (1) small house churches versus megachurches or numerically bigger churches, (2) most unreached versus responsive peoples or fields, and (3) volunteers from the harvest versus more missionaries.[35] Elaborating on his first point Garrison argues,

In my CPMs book I wrote: "First, the Church Growth Movement has come to associate

bigger churches with better churches." You will note that I do not attribute this to McGavran but rather to what the CGM "came to associate".

While the mega-church tendency could not be ascribed to Donald McGavran, who always had a heart for the frontiers and the unreached, it certainly did (as I wrote) apply to "the Church Growth Movement" that followed which did, in fact, come to associate "bigger churches with better churches" In the years <u>following</u> McGavran, the Church Growth Movement was shepherded by many CGM advocates who, I believe, were distracted by the pressure to show pastors how to grow their churches larger. Looking at the writings of Win Arn and Peter Wagner, there was a strong impulse to grow churches larger. Wagner, in particular, drew his models from many of the mega churches of Latin America and Korea as paragons to be emulated in the Church Growth Movement. Though this was not McGavran's emphasis—and I do not ascribe it to him—it did become the next wave of the Church Growth Movement, advocated from advocates Arn and Wagner and aggressively pursued particularly in those countries where Christianity had a long history (i.e. the U.S., Latin America, and Korea).

> *McGavran was not against growing churches larger, but (it seems to me) McGavran was always more concerned with reaching the lost through multiplication and movements: something I applaud. In fact, I see the CPM paradigm to be a much closer adherence to McGavran's original ideals.*[36]

Venn Middleton, an authority on McGavran's life and ministry, points out that Garrison is correct by not associating the megachurch movement with McGavran. While McGavran taught that congregations could take any form, he seemed to prefer small groups to enhance a speedy, and broad-reaching presentation of the gospel.[37]

McGavran focused on multiplication, a regularly repeated term in his classic *Understanding Church Growth*. As Garrison notes in the above quote, Wagner and Arn took the CGM into a different direction by associating Church Growth with megachurches.

Although Wagner pioneered the application of Church Growth principles within the American context, Elmer Towns and then John Vaughan vigorously pushed for megachurches within the CGM. Gary McIntosh elaborates,

> *Elmer Towns was the very first person to document the impact of megachurches. He wrote what is likely the first church growth book on North American churches titled The Ten Largest Sunday Schools (1969), which*

was followed by America's Fastest Growing Churches *(1972),* Great Soul Winning Churches *(1973), and* 10 of Today's Most Innovative Churches *(1990). Town's also authored a couple of books on Thomas Road Baptist Church (Jerry Falwell), which was also documenting a megachurch.*

However, it was John Vaughan who started the Megachurch Research Center in Bolivar, MO. He is the one who started tracking the 100 largest churches in the USA. He teamed with Elmer Towns on a couple of books in the late 1980s and early 1990s, and then wrote his own book Megachurches & America's Cities: How Churches Grow *(1993). Since those days, there has [sic] been a lot of books and writers on the megachurch, but these two men were the pioneers that ran with Wagner's ideas applying CG theory within the American context.*

On a side note, McGavran was never enamored with the megachurch. Rather, what he was interested in was churches that effectively made disciples through conversion growth. McGavran wrote to John Vaughan thanking John for his work on mega churches but asking John to document if megachurches were growth via conversion growth. McGavran had a hunch that many megachurches (not all) were growing primarily via transfer growth.[38]

Middleton also points out that some of the churches being planted were more Western in structure and ecclesiology as McGavran was more concerned that people were coming to Christ and gathered into congregations than the type of church building or the form of ecclesiology.[39]

Garrison offers additional clarity regarding the distinctions presented in his book:

> His [McGavran's] energy and frankly scientific approach to missions is very consistent with the early approach to missions that led to the CPM breakthroughs in our own organization. This is why it was so surprising to me (and continues to be) that so many of the critics of CPMs have claimed to be "Harvest Missiologists" and or Church Growth missiologists. These guys viewed our CPM endeavors among the world's least reached, as a waste of limited resources that should, instead, be limited to a "probing presence". They ardently advocated pouring resources into proven harvest fields such as Brazil and the Philippines rather than tackling the least reached, despite the fact that CPMs were primarily occurring among these same least reached peoples.[40]

So what is the CPM all about? Garrison argues that CPMs are the "most effective means in the world today for drawing lost millions into saving, disciple-building relationships with

Jesus Christ."[41] A movement is ultimately a divine work of God, but God also delegates a role to humans. Church multipliers can learn and practice the principles that enhance the chances for a CPM. Garrison argues that if movements are entirely an act of God, then God is to blame if a movement does not occur.[42] He goes on to say,

> *The question we face is not whether Church Planting Movements are right or wrong, but whether we will be participants or observers—allowing God's movement to pass by. God's handiwork in these movements are irrefutable as these movements are inevitable; it is we who are the question mark.*[43]

Table 1 summarizes the distinctive features representative of each evolution of Church Growth theory through the various eras of modern missions.

TABLE 1
THE CONTRIBUTIONS OF PIONEERS TO CHURCH GROWTH THEORY

Growth Theory & Pioneers of the Era	Geopolitical Context	Unique Contribution to Church Growth Theory
Indigenous movements		
Nevius Warneck Keysser Allen	Colonial period characterized by Western domination. Most Christians are Europeans. Missions is West to the rest.	Indigenization and group conversion

Church growth movements

Pickett McGavran Tippett Winter Wagner	Post-colonial period. Eclipse of Western domination. Rapid spread of Christianity around the globe. Emergence of non-western missions.	How people convert, i.e., people movements, homogeneous unit principle (HUP)

Church planting movement

Garrison	Geopolitical power shifting to Asia. Christianity is a non-western religion. Death of Christianity in the West. Center of Christianity shifting to the global south. Missions is a global movement.	Factors contributing to how churches multiply

LOOKING FORWARD FROM BEHIND

Our walk through the annals of missiological history revealed the minds and godly passions of great people of faith. Their unwavering faith in the will of God as revealed in Scripture forged their passion, believing that God fully intended to fulfill his plans to reconcile all nations to himself. From out of all the nations, God is creating a new nation—the people of God.

A question arises: Is there new ground to plow in relation to multiplication methodology? I believe there is. As reviewed in the last two chapters, an evolution of thought and praxis regarding multiplication and movements over the past three eras of missions has occurred.

Other related questions arise: Can the argument for multiplication and movements be advanced? Should another term be coined to describe this evolution? Can new aims be described more precisely while honoring the profound wisdom garnered from the cauldron of missionary effort and sacrifice over the past 200-plus years? Can missiologists build on research analysis rather than anecdotes? Has missions entered a fourth era that calls for a new type of pioneer who operates under a new model? Chapter 4 will begin to consider the last question.

CHAPTER 4

A FOURTH ERA of MISSIONS?

Have the Third Era missions leaders—Cameron Townsend and Donald McGavran—passed the baton to a new generation of strategists? Have the passing of time and the influence of globalization demanded a new type of cross-cultural Christian worker for a new era? A new selection criteria? New training requirements? New models and strategies? New missionary roles? Has a fourth era of missions emerged?

This chapter begins with a review of Ralph Winter's three eras of modern missions. It will also consider geopolitical changes within each era that provides the context in helping Christian workers to understand how missiological principles and practices emerged within each era. I follow this with a quick review of the major players in the Third Era, and then identify how global changes helped redirect IMB's models and strategies for multiplication and movements.

THREE MISSION ERAS

Ralph Winter summarized 200 years of modern Protestant missions history in what he called "eras of missions history." For each of the three eras, Winter identified a specific timeframe, a key individual(s) that defined the time period, and specific characteristics that distinguished one era from another even as some aspects continued from era to era (see Table 2).

TABLE 2
THREE ERAS OF THE PROTESTANT MODERN MISSIONARY MOVEMENT [1]

Modern Mission Eras	Key Individual(s)	Characteristics
First: 1800-1910	William Carey	European dominance focused on coastal cities.
Second: 1865-1980	Hudson Taylor	American dominance focused on the inlands.
Third: 1935-2000	Cameron Townsend, Donald McGavran	Lessening of Western dominance. Focus on unreached peoples.

The Protestant missionary movement emerged within the context of many geopolitical changes. One could describe the movement as HIStory in the midst of human history.

In the late 18th century two evangelical awakenings occurred within the United States and Great Britain that provided impetus for mobilizing Western Protestant churches to take the Great Commission seriously. A young British

Christian, William Carey, became cognizant of the secular forces spreading capitalism around the globe through various trading companies. He believed that one could harness similar means to spread the gospel, so, he launched the First Era of modern missions around 1800. Europeans predominated the thrust, focusing on reaching coastal cities.

During the first half of the 19th century, another young British missionary to China recognized God's call to take the gospel beyond the coastal regions to reach the inlands. Hudson Taylor began the China Inland Mission in 1865 while in the United Kingdom. The birth of China Inland Mission launched what became popularly known as the Faith Missions movement. Winter identified Taylor as the main figure in the Second Era. Eventually, North Americans dominated the Second Era as a result of evangelical fervor in the United States led by the likes of D. L. Moody.

In the Third Era of modern missions, Cameron Townsend and Donald McGavran, played key roles, beginning around 1935. God used these North Americans to focus the Church's attention on reaching hidden people groups (unreached people groups) through Bible translation and church planting. During this era, the missionary enterprise evolved into a global movement out of which the CGM would emerge.

THE SECOND AND THIRD ERAS AND THE CHURCH GROWTH MOVEMENT

Key players that helped develop the CGM included: John Nevius, Roland Allen, J. Waskom Pickett, Donald McGavran,

A. R. Tippett, Ralph Winter, Charles Kraft, and Peter Wagner. Trevor McIlwain, an Australian associated with New Tribes Mission, could also be added to this illustrious list although he would not consider himself part of the CGM.

Nevius advocated that evangelism and church planting be done through indigenous means rather than by local workers hired by expatriates. The Three-Selfs worked because they were practical.

Allen argued that the Three-Selfs worked, not because they were just practical, but because they were based on Pauline principles. They originated from the New Testament.

Pickett advocated evangelism that called for an entire community to come to Christ as a whole group, calling for mass movements. Methods mattered if indigeneity was to result.

McGavran, coming from a sociological perspective, believed that non-westerners preferred to come to Christ through homogeneous units, which he considered bridges of God, rather than one-by-one. He advocated genuine research, not fluid figures.

Tippett, looking through the eyes of history, anthropology, and theology, also advocated people group movements. Tippett considered missionary roles and methods central to indigenous church growth. He also filled a great vacuum by writing a theology of church growth in *Church Growth and the Word of God: The Biblical Basis of the Church Growth Viewpoint.*

Winter provided a schematic for the various modern mission eras while advancing the concept of unreached people groups in multiple ways. The USCWM served (and serves) as a missions Pentagon, a centralized missions headquarters for reaching unreached people groups around the world.

Charles Kraft recognized the need for each people group to develop its own theology as Western theology often failed to consider local cultural needs. His ground-breaking book entitled *Christianity in Culture: A Study in Dynamic Biblical Theologizing in Cross-Cultural Perspective* stirred great debate among evangelicals. He also pioneered in the area of spiritual warfare believing that the CGM failed to consider this central dimension of Christianity.

Wagner helped systematize Church Growth principles through his numerous books and articles, and like Kraft, added spiritual warfare. He also refocused the CGM to building bigger and stronger churches rather than multiplying them.

McIlwain, following up a people movement among the Palawanos in the Philippines, soon discovered that although many claimed to be "Christians," they did not understand the gospel. To challenge the syncretism, McIlwain designed a comprehensive curriculum first entitled the Chronological Bible Teaching model, and later Firm Foundations. His story approach to evangelism and discipleship went global, first among tribal peoples, and then among urbanites.[2]

McIlwain based his approach on the fact that,

> *Insufficient time is generally given to teach the Old Testament background and foundations for the Gospel. Syncretism of heathen and Christian beliefs is often the sad result. Many in foreign lands who have professed Christianity do not understand the Gospel and the Scriptures as one book. Many missionaries are so eager to preach the gospel that they feel it is an unnecessary waste of time to teach tribal people too much of the historical portions of the Old Testament scriptures.*[3]

He believed that "healthy churches result from a correct understanding of the gospel."[4]

McIlwain designed a seven-phase church planting model integrating chronological teaching with church planting. Later, Henry Sheffield developed *Tribal Strategy Chart with Explanatory Notes,* a visual guide based off of Steffen's five-stage model that integrates chronological teaching with church planting, Bible translation, and community development. Mark Zook also wrote a book to aid in understanding the application of McIlwain's principles entitled *Church Planting Step by Step.*

Although McIlwain would not include himself in the CGM, his significant contribution in providing structure that integrated chronological teaching and church planting to launch a healthy CPM in rural and urban areas should not go overlooked.

These pivotal figures helped move the Protestant missions into and beyond the Third Era, during which time Church Growth principles were clearly systematized, crystalizing the CGM. Table 3 summarizes their contributions.

TABLE 3
CHURCH GROWTH CONTRIBUTIONS BY SECOND AND THIRD ERA MISSIONARIES

Key Figures	CGM Contributions
Nevius	Three Selfs work because practical
Allen	Three Selfs work because biblical
Pickett	Role of missionary / Methods matter Mass movement conversions Indigenization
McGavran	People movements Homogeneous Unit Principle Indigenization Research
Tippett	Group conversions Indigenization Theology of Church Growth
Winter	USCWM Unreached people groups
Kraft	Ethnotheology Spiritual warfare

Wagner	Systemizes church growth principles Spiritual warfare
McIlwain	Story approach that lays a firm gospel foundation to produce healthy church growth

GLOBALIZATION CHALLENGES MISSIONS

External factors within each era impinged on church expansion methodology. For example, a majority of the time since the inception of the modern missionary movement launched by Carey, up until about 1960, Western European countries colonized much of the world. This external geopolitical factor affected the way missionaries conducted missions. Typically, the West viewed their ways as superior, therefore missions entailed both Christianizing and civilizing.

Webb Keane's *Christian Moderns: Freedom & Fetish in the Mission Encounter* is helpful here: "Well into the twentieth century, Protestantism was a thoroughly familiar part of the moral, political, and conceptual world in much of the Euro-American West, even for the most unreligious."[5] He points out, "At the beginning of the twenty-first century, one-third of the world's population is Christian, and that one-third of those Christians live in former colonies."[6] Within this milieu, predominantly Western missionaries carried out their mission work.

World events continued to evolve rapidly. Communist countries like China shifted to free market economies, rapidly emerging as a competing super power to the United States. Americans and Europeans continued to build debt, bringing some Western economies to the brink of financial collapse. Results from the 2012 Arab Spring remain undetermined as to whether or not radical Islam will ultimately prevail over democratic forces. And a global missionary movement sent short-termers and long-termers from everywhere to everywhere.

With all these changing circumstances, especially with the geopolitical axis of power shifting away from the West, how should Western missions respond? The geopolitical context that birthed much of the CGM no longer exists. What is the role of Western missions? Does a church planting model exist that incorporates advances from the CGM while at the same time incorporating what is being learned from CPMs?

Steffen, another key figure in this emerging era, offers in his book *The Facilitator Era* a prophetic tenor for these rapidly changing times. Building on Winter's three eras of modern missions, he proposes that Western missions *has* moved beyond the Third Era of McGavran and Townsend who focused on reaching UPGs.

Steffen proposes that McGavran and Townsend have passed the baton to new leadership representing a Fourth Era that requires a new selection profile, new training, and new models and strategies for church multiplication. In short, a new era requires a new type of missionary with a different ministry focus.

Rather than going to reach the unreached, as in the Third Era, Western missionary representatives of the Fourth Era will focus primarily on influencing the reached to reach the unreached. Steffen elaborates,

> The Fourth Era is the shift from unreached to reached peoples. The majority of Western missionaries used to go directly to unreached people groups, but they have begun going primarily to the already reached. They go to the discipled rather than to the undiscipled, and then they partner with them in a multitude of ways to reach the unreached people groups.[7]

And they will accomplish this by facilitating "existing national church-planting movements in multiple ways."[8] Interestingly Smith and Kai make a similar point.

> Perhaps the single most important start you can make to a CPM strategy utilizing T4T is to mobilize believers from within your context or from a near-culture people group. Mobilization means that you cast vision to these believers about what God can do in and through them and then begin to train those who agree to walk forward in the T4T process.[9]

IMB MAKES CHANGES

In *Church Planting Movements,* Garrison described the IMB's efforts to evangelize and church plant among specific people groups. IMB launched a rapid-advance team to place missionaries among people groups living within restricted access countries (RAC). The idea of the nonresidential missionary was born. Eventually they were called "Strategy Coordinators." Their job? Complete the evangelization of their specific people group.

As a new era dawned, new strategies and methods were demanded. SCs were forced to adopt catalytic and modeling roles (in contrast to a pioneer role) where indigenous principles were highly emphasized for the purpose of seeing the complete evangelization of people groups through the rapid multiplication of churches, a CPM. As this new breed of missionaries forged ahead under very difficult circumstances, principles were learned that God seemed to honor. Within a relatively short period of time, thousands of new churches were reportedly multiplying throughout various people groups.[10]

NOW WHERE?

These developments raise a number of strategic questions pertinent to the Fourth Era. Should another term besides CPM be coined to describe this evolution? Can missiologists build on analysis rather than anecdotes? Are there models out there that clearly combine the best of the CGM and CPM? Do these models address the various criticisms of CPMs? Will these models produce sustainable CPMs? By sustainable, I mean: (1) a movement that reproduces healthy churches and leaders to at least the fourth generation with multiple streams, and

(2) believers being transformed by the Holy Spirit, living in and transforming communities, and obeying the commands of Christ until Jesus' return.

Before suggesting a possible new model that addresses some of the various questions raised above, Chapter 5 will categorize the concerns and criticisms of CPMs leveled by critics.

CHAPTER 5

CPM CONCERNS & CRITICISMS

Chapter 1 highlighted some of the concerns and criticisms of CPMs leveled by various critics. In this chapter I will expand on these, categorizing them under the four legs of missiology: missions history, social sciences, theology, and strategy. Some concerns and critiques will overlap in the four legs due to the integrative nature of missiology.

MISSIOLOGY

Charles Taber defined missiology as the "critical reflection on the task of mission."[1] It is the "conscious, intentional, ongoing reflection on the doing of mission."[2] Missiology, an eclectic, integrated, relatively young discipline of some 160 years, takes seriously a number of disciplines.

One of the disciplines that missiology takes seriously is missions history. Why? Because the study of "individuals being brought to God in history"[3] provides honed ministry principles and practices for future generations.

Another discipline, anthropology, originated from the social sciences. Anthropology helps Christian workers to better understand the worldviews of people groups, including their own.

Theology comprised the third discipline. Theologians systematized understanding of Scripture, providing motive, message, and methods.

These three disciplines impact and drive the final leg, strategy. This is where CPMs fit in. One's depth of understanding and integration of missions history, anthropology, and theology will influence CPM strategy positively or negatively. By overlooking or minimizing any of the three, and by beginning ministry with strategy, one can get into trouble very fast.

MISSIONS HISTORY

Concerns related to missions history touch on a number of areas. First, is there a historical basis for movements? In Chapter 2, I briefly explored the historical evidence found in Scripture. For example, the book of Acts recorded numerous examples of movements that typically emphasized large numbers of believers being added to the Church. As the gospel spread from the Jewish Church in Jerusalem, the Church continued to expand throughout Judea, Samaria, and, ultimately, to the ends of the Roman Empire. This spontaneous expansion of the Church directly fulfilled Jesus' promise found in Acts 1:8.

Acts 9:31 recorded how the Church increased in numbers as advocates preached the gospel throughout Judea, Galilee, and Samaria (Acts 11:21; 14:21; 16:5). The Church continued to add numbers even among those from the Gentile world, an area currently encompassing modern Turkey and Eastern Europe. Eventually, the gospel reached as far east as Spain. In each account, the biblical record emphasized large numbers being added to the Church (Acts 19:8-10, 26; 28:30-31). In Romans 15:23-24, Paul implies that within 30 years of ministry (35AD-65AD), pioneer church planting in these regions was completed so that his motivation shifted to Spain!

This Spirit-led movement ignited by the preaching of the gospel of Jesus, a Jew from Nazareth, had such an impact on the Roman Empire that by as early as A.D. 197 the famous early church apologist Tertullian wrote,

> *We are but of yesterday, and yet we have filled all the places that belong to you – cities, islands, forts, towns, exchanges, the military camps themselves, tribes, towns councils, the palace, the senate, the market-place; we have left you nothing but your temples.*[4]

Even secular leaders of the time took notice of the rapid change of events within the Roman Empire. Smith and Kai pointed out that Pliny, the governor of the distant province of Bithynia, in a letter to the emperor Trajan (A.D. 111), highlighted the great number of people from a wide spectrum of society that were part of the Christian movement. "For many persons of every age, every rank, and also of both sexes are and will be endangered. For the contagion of this superstition has spread not only to the cities but also the villages and farms."[5]

Although the Spirit-led writers of Scripture (2 Pet. 1:21) never described a specific ministry model used in the movement, nor identified the movement as a PM or CPM, I surmise that this movement had elements of both. What is abundantly clear, however, is that a dramatic movement did take place. Paul hints at the core of his strategy in 2 Timothy 2:2, "The things you have heard me say in the presence of many witnesses entrust to reliable men who will also be qualified to teach others."

In Chapter 2, I provided historical examples from the first millennium during which time Europe was being evangelized. Patrick of Ireland and Boniface of Crediton were key figures of this period.

For the late 19th and then 20th centuries, I focused particularly on the past 200 years, delineating the modern era of missions in which Protestants played a prominent role. During that time, numerous individuals emerged, especially those from the CGM—Pickett, McGavran, Tippett—who compiled convincing evidence that PMs indeed have historical precedence. Table 4 summarizes the concerns and critiques leveled against CPMs from the historical perspective.

TABLE 4
CPM CONCERNS AND CRITICISMS RELATED TO MISSIONS HISTORY

Does the biblical record, particularly Acts, provide evidence of movements that were rapid, incorporating large numbers of new converts?

Is speedy multiplication consistent with Pauline teams?

Is there historical evidence of movements outside of Scripture? Were they considered good?

Does history show that movements are a natural feature for people groups entering Christianity?

SOCIAL SCIENCES: ANTHROPOLOGY

Garrison seems to have taken a dim view of the linguistic and anthropological advances made in the missionary community over the past 100 years. Further, his writings do not encourage incarnational ministry or contextualization.

Interestingly, this lack of concern for anthropological issues contradicts what I discovered during field interviews. For example, while discussing worldview, the International Director of Evangelization of a large international missions agency believed that one did not have a legitimate movement if worldview had not been adequately addressed. Additionally, senior missionaries that lived very close to their host group emphasized that missionaries should understand the many issues related to culture for the purpose of providing a biblical response. One missionary with New Tribes Mission emphasized how difficult it was to go back and fix things if a firm foundation for the gospel had not been laid.

In light of this, one wonders if CPMs are steeped in the American values of expediency and pragmatism? Does the need for speed and practicality demand ignoring all the cultural and worldview challenges that should be addressed in an emerging and ongoing church movement? Does anthropology have any direct contribution to the way CPMs are birthed? Maintained? Remain authentic? Remain sustainable? Garrison seems to be redefining pioneer mission praxis. Table 5 summarizes some key questions related to anthropological concerns and critiques.

TABLE 5
CPM CONCERNS AND CRITICISMS RELATED TO THE SOCIAL SCIENCES

Why is incarnational ministry downplayed?

What role should culture and language acquisition play for the expatriate? Locals?

What role should contextualization have?

How indigenous are the churches?

What indigenous symbols and rituals will require Christian substitutes?

How well do expatriates understand the economic system so that dependency does not result?

How well do expatriates understand the social system so that they know how Christianity will spread?

How well do expatriates understand the political system so that they know what governance looks like on multiple levels?

How well do they understand the host culture's pedagogical preferences so that they can communicate effectively?

How well do expatriates understand the local worldview so that they can identify bridges and barriers for initial evangelism?

How well do expatriates understand the local worldview so that worldview transformation is maximized?

THEOLOGY

All praxis must be weighed in light of Scripture. Concerns and criticisms center around four theological areas: (1) a biblical basis for CPMs, (2) the definition of a local church, (3) ecclesiology, and (4) the gospel message.

Ample Scripture exists to support CPMs, as noted above. Scripture supports such movements as part of God's plan for redeeming mankind.

A second line of questions relates to the definition of a local church. To a great extent, one's definition of "church" determines the size, spiritual maturity, Bible curricula covered, speed of multiplication, the type, levels, and qualifications of leadership, training, use of the sacraments, addressing the phases of life, such as, birth, death, and marriage, and so forth.

I define a church as a group of born again Christ disciples that self identify as a local community of believers representing Christ to those around them, carrying out the three-fold ministry of worship, ministering the Word and spiritual gifts within the body, and fulfilling the Great Commission. Though these characteristics may not be fully evident within a newly formed group of believers, they should be growing and maturing towards fulfilling these qualities of a local church.

Curtis Sergeant, who as a strategy coordinator has seen hundreds of groups started, defines church as, "the presence of Jesus among His people, called out as a spiritual family to live in obedience to their Lord's commands and pursue His purposes on earth."[6]

J.D. Payne, formerly the Director of the Billy Graham School for Missions and Evangelism at Southern Seminary, and presently the Pastor for Church Multiplication at The Church at Brook Hills in Alabama, defines church as,

> …a regenerate baptized body of believers that self identify themselves to be the local expression of the Universal body of Christ. They are living out the kingdom ethic in their relationships toward God, toward other kingdom citizens, and toward those that are outside the kingdom."[7]

As noted above, a fully mature group of believers displaying all the biblical characteristics of a church does not happen immediately. So the question becomes, what would be a good threshold that characterizes new church plants, particularly within the context of a movement? Curtis Sergeant is helpful here, emphasizing that the early priorities of a local group of believers, i.e., church, should be the following:

1. Develop regular cycles of dual accountability within the church (to apply what the Lord teaches them and to pass it on to others.)
2. Equip disciples to be self-feeding so they can be producers and not merely consumers. This includes the areas of:
    a. Interpreting and applying Scripture (which is a major way they can obey "all that Christ commanded.")
    b. Prayer (including listening prayer, prayer without ceasing, teaching prayer, evangelistic prayer, as well as the "regular" emphases on patterns of prayer [like the Lord's prayer] and intercession.)
    c. Body life (such as an awareness of the "one another" passages and an understanding of the way the body functions through spiritual gifts, etc.)
    d. Persecution and suffering (so they are not discouraged or bitter when they face these but can be intentional in looking to capitalize on the opportunity for growth, equipping, and learning.)
3. Help them develop "eyes to see where the Kingdom isn't" so they look for the gaps, the dark places, the places where the Lord needs to break in and break through.
4. Help them steward their existing network of relationships well for the Kingdom AND know how to establish beachheads in "foreign" places through locating and discipling people of peace.[8]

The WHEEL MODEL

J.D. Payne offers some additional helpful insights on how one embeds the necessary DNA for a sustained movement to occur.

> The missionaries need to have in mind some set things that they are going to be teaching these people as they move forward by helping those people in understanding what the body of Christ is supposed to be about at a local level. So I think a team needs to have that as part of their teaching and modeling before the people. It includes things like worship and ministry and prayer and what it means to be in community in living with each other and what it means to be on mission. So the classical self governing, self supporting, self propagating, self teaching, self expressing, self identifying need to be in place when the church is birthed. But the way those things look in those early days will look very different 3-5 years down the road.
>
> So one of my concerns along those lines is that missionaries will often read books on ecclesiology that are written by solid Bible teachers who are often times pastors or theologians but are written in the context of a well established church. So they think that OK just because the NT Church has these different characteristics, these 5 these 10

> *different characteristics, marks or whatever, therefore we have to have all these things in place immediately. So if we don't see them immediately we're not a Church. I would say that those things develop over time out of context so there needs to be intentionality in moving that direction but at the same time recognizing that in the beginning that the church will be very simple and very basic.*[9]

I completely agree. This discussion brings to mind an interaction I had with a local tribal believer in North Thailand back in the mid-90s. He explained to me that our team of missionaries constantly emphasized obedience to what they were being taught from Scripture. While he agreed that Jesus and Scripture demanded obedience, he went on to explain that sometimes they just needed a little time to figure out how to be obedient within the milieu of their community. So much of Scripture was counter cultural and he expressed the fact that some time was needed to apply Scripture while at the same time maintaining their communal relationships so the gospel would still have an open door to spread naturally within their village and clan.

Interestingly, this opened up an entirely new conversation about cultural substitutes and redeeming parts of their culture. The discussion was raised to a far higher level than when I was learning contexualization principles in seminary, or from other missionaries! Though I believe immediate obedience is a priority that should be emphasized, this inside look was eye opening to me as a young tribal missionary.

A related concern is ecclesiology in relation to social ministries. In the above paragraphs, I alluded to the fact that Christ calls his Church to be the central agent of change for redeeming culture and society so that his Father's will will be done on earth as it is in heaven (Matthew 6:10).

Payne defines ecclesiology simply as, "the study of the doctrine of the Church."[10] Bryan Stone offers a more comprehensive theological definition: "Ecclesiology is a discipline that undertakes critical and constructive reflection on the Christian community as a distinct social body in the world and as a particular people in history."[11]

But how does this doctrine apply to everyday church planting, especially within a pioneer context where many groups and churches are expected to emerge and multiply within a people group? Typically these people have no history with the gospel, the Bible, or with church. In fact, many UPGs do not even have a Bible in their own language. So practical questions often asked among church planters engaged in CPMs are: How do I gather new believers? What form should the meeting take? How does one get a group going so that they can mature spiritually so that they can truly represent Christ in the local area in which they live? In other words, now that people are believing in Christ, what does one do with them?

Ultimately, one's definition of ecclesiology must answer the "how," "what," "where," and "whom" questions, some of which were noted above. Most church planters come from more established churches, so they often do not have a mental picture that relates to a pioneer situation. This creates a serious obstacle that must be addressed. Therefore, start simple, realizing that there is a maturing process. One mistake I often observe among new workers is that they are far too passive. Exercising initiative and being intentional is often far more effective. This DNA should be modeled and passed on to new believers immediately.

Garrison believes that it is critical to address ecclesiology in order to see sustained movements. All participants in the research recognized that ultimately, healthy, biblically-sound churches are the priority. J.D. Payne, an authority on ecclesiology, offers helpful insights:

> *The new believers are now following His [Jesus'] leadership as their King and they are going to live out the kingdom ethic that is found in His word that teaches them how to live in covenant community with one another. It also teaches them how to live in relationship with those outside the kingdom.*[12]

A local church participating in social ministries is a key aspect of church planting that must be taken seriously. The central question is, *who* will do this ministry? Should it be the local group of believers? Or as is far too common, a group of believers from half way around the world with missionaries being the conduit? Though my thinking is constantly being challenged on this topic, my present position is that it is the responsibility of local believers as much as possible! Of course circumstances influence the extent of their responses. I have observed first hand that the impact among non-believers is far greater when local believers take this responsibility.

Two examples come to mind. I remember one village that experienced a fire during the time of year when fields are burnt off to get ready for the rainy season and planting. In this particular instance, the wind shifted and almost the entire village was burned to the ground as a result. Interestingly when the fire reached the church building, the flames suddenly went around the church and continued to burn all the other structures around it! But that is another story!

After the fire it was very interesting how the believers from numerous surrounding villages, though poor, took responsibility to help the destroyed village. They gathered an offering and also received some government aid while at the same time worked through the non-believing headman of the village. I attended but stayed in the background while the church leaders gave out aid to both believers and *unbelievers* equally, all while emphasizing that they, believers and unbelievers alike, are part of the same community.

A second story also comes to mind when communist soldiers and police attacked numerous Hmong villages in Laos near the Thai border. Believers, especially leaders, were targeted and needed to immediately flee their homes. Some leaders were reportedly murdered as well.

Though I did not live in that area anymore during the time of the attack, I received the news of what was going on through the local missionary. We immediately set up a project to channel funds from outside donors. This was an international incident so we believed an international response was appropriate. But at the same time, local believers were the conduit to provide helping hands and feet to the persecuted believers as they swam across the treacherous waters of the Mekong River. The immediate needs of the fleeing believers were quickly met through the helping hands of fellow believers from around the world, but the local believers were still the faces and voices offering direct help. Some believers even took some families in, helping them set up a new life in Thailand. Their compassion cost them personal time and money.

Payne, as does Garrison, understands that the local church and it's role in society is deeply rooted in ecclesiology. Payne goes on to say that, "in the push to make disciples in which we try to reach the many, we at times forget that Jesus has called us to also teach them to obey all that he has commanded." Elaborating more fully he goes on to say that,

> *You know part of the problem stems from the missionaries and their work. I have read and I have heard of people saying, well myself and another missionary in an evangelistic bible study in someone's home or in someone's apartment constitutes the Church.*

> *And I would say that that is absolutely not the case. You know it may be a preaching point, it may be an evangelistic Bible study but there is more to the church than just 2 or 3 gathered together in Jesus' name.*[13]

So how do we encourage a movement where healthy churches are planted and good ecclesiology is practiced? Both my research and personal experience show that initially it is important to follow the precedent set by the CGM and CPM, i.e., making evangelism and church planting a high priority. Churches born out of this philosophy are then responsible to obey the Great Commandment, i.e., loving their neighbors. Local churches, rather than congregations half way around the world, take the primary responsibility to meet the social needs around them.

A final aspect of theology in the context of sustainable church multiplication movements is the gospel message and how it is presented. Numerous participants focused on presenting the metanarrative of Scripture to help effect worldview transformation. They believed an accurate understanding of the gospel is essential because "the seeds of destruction are inherent in any presentation of the gospel message."[14] This should supersede rapid multiplication.[15] Steffen addresses this concern when he says, "If you mess up the message, you mess up the movement."[16]

At a Thai worship service I attended recently a Thai pastor from Bangkok was just finishing a three-day CPM training, climaxing in the final worship service. After the service I spoke with him and found out that he was trained by Bill Smith and had read Thai translations of Garrison's *Church Planting Movements* as well as Steve Smiths and Ying Kai's *T4T*. It had affected his thinking dramatically so now he was training other trainers!

One aspect of his final presentation that really struck me was his emphasis on who Jesus Christ is and his kingdom purposes. It was after that was established that he then went on to stress CPMs. Movements are a natural outgrowth of our intimate relationship with Christ! I believe this recent example helps address Steffen's concern of message and movement.

All experienced CPM practitioners in the research wished to see the gospel transform lives. However, not all addressed worldview concerns in the same way. For example, some CPM practitioners focused on a more systematic teaching presentation of the metanarrative of Scripture through Chronological Bible Teaching while others simply told Bible stories. During post-story dialogue, they referred all questions raised by local believers back to Scripture. All participants, however, focused on obedience-based training rather than knowledge-based. Table 6 serves as a summary of theological concerns and criticisms.

TABLE 6
CPM CONCERNS AND CRITICISMS RELATED TO THEOLOGY

Does Scripture support large numbers of people converting to Christianity within a short period of time?
Does the definition of church meet biblical standards?
What is the role of ecclesiology in sustaining a movement?

The WHEEL MODEL

How Western is their ecclesiology?

How well do they understand hermeneutics?

How much social transformation takes place within society?

How much foundation for the gospel is laid?

Does an accurate gospel challenge each generation's worldview through bridges and barriers?

How well does each generation capture the metanarrative of Scripture?

If Scripture is unavailable, how is it provided? Is translation part of the strategy?

Have reciprocators captured missions or just evangelism?

During evangelism, is the gospel presentation focused on an honor-shame framework rather than guilt-innocence, as is typical in the West?

What theological curricula are planned? Who develops it? Who disperses?

How does an expatriate handle the spirit world and the signs and wonders taking place within a people group when one's theology does not address them?

Does the discipleship phase have adequate depth to sustain a movement for four generations?

How are symbols, rituals, and phases of life contextualized so that Christianity becomes a total way of life?

Has each generation of the movement avoided extensive syncretism?

Does regeneration accompany each generation?

Who trains potential leadership in each generation of the movement?

What is the role of Bible schools?

STRATEGY

The line of questions related to strategy concerns and criticisms centers primarily on the legitimacy of speedy multiplication, the role of the missionary, and the role of local believers.

Evidence gathered during the research demonstrated that rapid movements have mixed results. Sustained movements tended to focus on training local leaders and encouraging churches to develop their own indigenous ecclesiology.

The role of the missionary to provide adequate modeling was another area of concern. Some experienced CPM practitioners have/had very distant relationships with locals while others learned the language and culture, thereby giving them stronger working relationships with the locals. What the appropriate role will be for the cross-cultural worker remains to be seen as missions moves further into the Fourth Era. All the participants interviewed aimed at indigenizing the work from the start, including funding.

At a recent meeting of the International Jonathan Executive Committee made up of Jonathan Coordinators from various regions of the world, Sergeant, who was an invited consultant because of his vast knowledge and experience working with CPMs around the world, noted, "In the movements I've seen, the outsider takes very much a back seat role."[17]

Sergeant's quote raises a number of key questions related to CPMs. If true universally, how does this impact modeling and ongoing discipling of a movement? Does the minimalist role require a different sort of training in preparation for entering missionary service? See Table 7 for a summary of the concerns and critiques related to strategy.

TABLE 7
CPM CONCERNS AND CRITICISMS RELATED TO STRATEGY

Are CPMs driven by foreign funds, thereby making them unsustainable long-term? How reproducible is the expatriate model?

Who models the ideal to the locals in each generation of church planting? To what extent?

Do expatriates use indigenous pedagogical styles? Do locals when they minister cross-culturally?

How is leadership developed and multiplied generationally?

Does an exit strategy drive the expatriate?

What role should holistic ministry play in each generation?

How much do American Western values, such as efficiency and pragmatism, drive CPMs?

What role does ethnodoxology (worship songs/ordinances/lifecycle and calendric rituals/Bible translation, etc.) play?

What role do partnerships play so that a comprehensive Christianity is offered?

How do locals representing generations 2-4 view CPMs?

Dovetailing this research with Steffen's argument that modern missions has transitioned into a Fourth Era, the question of sustainability looms large. Reiterating his quote from Chapter 1, Steffen challenges the type of movement that should result:

> One common value you will hear today is the desire for a *sustainable movement*. This value raises another question: sustainable in what areas? If sustainable refers to just keeping the movement going, I would have some deep reservations. Keeping a movement going that includes mostly those who have experienced deep worldview transformation is one thing. Keeping a movement going without such transformation is a totally different matter.[18]

Elaborating further, Steffen argues that the term sustainability does not disclose the level of genuineness of the movement. Is it doing exceptional? Mediocre? Abysmal? Rather, it only concludes that the movement speedily (or not so speedily) marches along irrespective of its spiritual health.[19]

Sustainability begs the question as to the genuineness of a movement in every aspect. For this reason Steffen prefers to "speak of *authentic* CPMs rather than merely sustainable ones."[20] He concludes, "We must *make haste slowly* so that an authentic movement results, not just a sustainable movement."[21] Steffen makes a valid point that echoes the concerns of many critics.

Although Steffen prefers the term authentic over sustainable, I would argue that the Wheel Model presented in Chapter 6 includes an emphasis on sustainability that does answer his (and others) question. The Wheel Model incorporates both multiplication through generational growth and the more enduring questions related to worldview transformation.

TIME FOR A NAME CHANGE?

The need for a model that promotes sustainable multiplication through generational growth is why I have moved away from the acronym CPM in favor of a new one, S-CMM (Sustainable Church Multiplication Movement). S-CMM is more comprehensive and answers the authentic question raised by Steffen and others who share his concern. More discussion on S-CMM will follow.

SUMMARY

Critics of modern day CPMs have highlighted numerous legitimate concerns and critiques. These demand and deserve attention so that spiritual generations become, and remain, strong and loyal in the Faith. What practitioners need today is a S-CMM model that addresses the concerns and criticisms raised in this chapter. Chapter 6 will propose such a model.

CHAPTER 6

THE WHEEL MODEL

Is a new CPM model required for the Fourth Era of missions? How should best practices that contribute to a sustainable CPM influence such a model?

From 2010 to 2012, I had the opportunity to mine the minds of 23 great mission thinkers and CPM practitioners. Participants were carefully selected who had extensive practical working knowledge with CPM methodology in Asia. Not all were experiencing huge movements, but all were successful at some level. Their years of ministry experience ranged from 15 to 40 plus.

During the interviews I asked them to define sustainability within the context of a CPM, followed by a series of questions that required specific answers about what they considered best practices necessary for sustainability. I then transcribed and analyzed their responses. From this data I formulated the Wheel Model defined below.

This chapter will move beyond description to prescription as it seeks to create a model that addresses the concerns and criticisms of critics while including best practices articulated by CPM practitioners during the interviews.

A PROPOSED MODEL

Three parts compose the proposed Wheel Model: the hub, the spokes, and the rim. Two elements comprise the hub: the Holy Spirit and vision. The spokes (fruitful practices) represent the practitioner's part in initiating and sustaining a CPM. The five fruitful practices include: mission, reproduction, worldview, church ecclesiology, and leadership. Finally, the rim includes four universals: prayer, training, indigenization, and modeling. All four universals factor into each of the five fruitful practices (see: Figure 1). See Appendix A for The Wheel Assessment Tool.

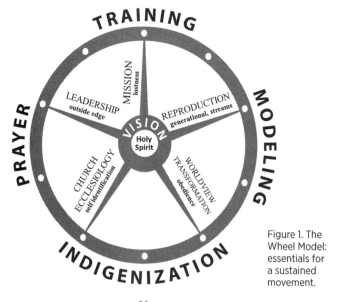

Figure 1. The Wheel Model: essentials for a sustained movement.

THE HUB

The hub of the wheel serves as the core. Without it, nothing happens.

At the very center of the hub is the Holy Spirit. Without the Spirit, one is not in co-mission with God to fulfill His mission. The core (Holy Spirit) can be compared to a car's axle as it connects the wheel to the power source. This is analogous to movements in that they are a sovereign work of God.

It would be a false assumption, however, to think that followers of Christ do not have an important and critical role in his sovereign work. CPMs are a unique divine-human relationship where God through the Holy Spirit is assumed to be the most reliable partner. The job for the people of God is to hoist the sails in the work of church planting so when the winds of the Holy Spirit begin to blow, a CPM can be birthed.

John Calvin, in his commentary on Malachi 4:6, highlights the same point:

> When God thus speaks highly of his ministers, the power of his Spirit is not excluded; and he shows how great is the power of truth when he works through it by the secret influence of his Spirit. God sometimes connects himself with his servants, and sometimes separates himself from them: when he connects himself with them, he transfers to them what never ceases to dwell in him; for he never resigns to them

> *his own office, but makes them partakers of it only.*[1]

Vision finds itself just outside the core of the Holy Spirit. The Holy Spirit's role in bringing about a movement is God's part; vision is our part as we agree with God to bring about movements to Christ. Both are highly interrelated (Prov. 16:1).

As Christ followers in co-mission with the Holy Spirit, our role is to grasp God's vision birthed in the Word of God and be empowered by the Holy Spirit. It is assumed that God desires every nation, tribe, people and language be reached so it is also assumed that the Holy Spirit is our most reliable partner. As the most reliable partner, he reinforces and strengthens the vision through a divine-human relationship. We share the very heart of God when we desire, pray for, and work towards the complete evangelization of every person on this planet.

Two historical examples come to mind. The first is James Fraser's work among the Lisu in SW China in the early 1900s. The second is Samuel Pollard's work among the Big Flowery Miao (Hmong), northwest of Kunming in the northern most part of Yunnan province. They were contemporaries and both saw an amazing move of God among these people. But what was the vision of these two men before they saw movements among the Lisu and Miao?

Fraser, of the CIM (presently OMF), pioneered alone among the remote and seemingly resistant Lisu. After years of fruitless efforts to reach these people, even to the point of giving up, a movement suddenly emerged! Geraldine Taylor recorded what happened in her book *Behind The Ranges*.

> It was some weeks after [Allyn] Cooke's return from the 'Cold Country' before the sequel to his visit became known, when one of the Lisu companions he had left behind turned up in Tengyueh, eager to find Fraser, with a long order for Gospels, hymn-books and catechisms. 'But who are they for?' was the natural question. 'Why, for all the converts in our Christian villages.' 'All the converts! Are they then so many?' 'Yes, scores of families. And more are coming in.'[2]

Was Fraser surprised by this news? No! This is what he said,

> I believe it was January 12, 1915, that I was definitely led to ask God for 'several hundreds of families' from the Lisu. Some may say, 'your prayer has at last been answered.' No! I took the answer then. I believed then that I had it. The realization has only now come, it is true, but God does not keep us waiting for answers. He gives them at once. Daniel 9.23.[3]

Fraser's vision agreed with the Holy Spirit's so he prayed the prayer of faith.

Samuel Pollard, a Methodist that worked very closely with James Adam of the CIM (OMF) also saw an amazing move of God that was even greater than was happening among the Lisu! W. A. Grist records the initial stages of this movement in his book *Samuel Pollard,* "After this a steady daily procession of Miao pilgrims came – scores, then hundreds until the citizens of Chaotong were moved with curiosity and then with alarm."[4]

Was Pollard surprised at this change of events about the Miao? He, like Fraser, prayed the prayer of faith years previously.

> Sixteen years had gone since Pollard wrote during a week of special prayer at Yunnan Fu. 'I had the promise at that meeting that we are going to have thousands of souls. Mind, I believe that from the bottom of my heart.' When the four Miao scouts came and told the missionaries of a whole tribe waiting for the new teaching, Pollard looked upon them as the first-fruits of the promised thousand.[5]

Both of these men joined the Holy Spirit in believing God for a movement among their host people. They pursued that vision by faith!

THE SPOKES

The spokes of a wheel provide the support that enables forward movement. The Wheel Model has five spokes, each described as a key result area (KRA). Each KRA is critical for a sustained movement, hence the label fruitful practices.

Each KRA has a critical success factor (CSF) that enables one to assess progress; it serves as the basic activity that will help move the work in the right direction so that eventually fruitful practices will become permanent fixtures in the work. Generally, CSFs serve as a necessary element to measure achievement for any organization or project.

In sports we call these the fundamentals. As is most often the case, the best athletes practice the fundamentals so that they become second nature. The focus, therefore, is not on the entire game, but perfecting the fundamentals so that eventually success is achieved in playing the game. Athletes and coaches are often heard saying, "Focus on the fundamentals and the victories will come." Church planters should train with a similar mindset.

So the five fruitful practices (KRAs) and the corresponding fundamentals that require focus include: 1) to achieve Mission, practice the fundamental of focusing on reaching the lost, 2) for Reproduction, practice the fundamental of achieving generational growth, 3) for Worldview Transformation, ask the fundamental question, is obedience to the Word being practiced? 4) for Ecclesiology/Church, ask the fundamental question, do the believers believe they self-identify as a group? and 5) for Leadership, ask the fundamental question, is the focus on immediately raising up lay leaders that will shepherd the emerging churches?

God is the church multipliers most reliable partner when working towards movements. According to Scripture he desires every person on this planet to come into his Kingdom. The weak link is often us, the church multiplier. So what are the fruitful practices and fundamentals that church multipliers must promote? The following section will provide a more detailed picture.

KRA/CSF # 1: Mission/Lostness

For a movement to begin and be sustained, the DNA of mission must be planted deep in the heart of everyone involved. It begins with the missionary, but the baton is quickly passed to the local believers who have the ability to multiply this DNA throughout the movement.

What does it mean to implant a missional DNA, the essential catalyst for a movement to begin? Understanding personal responsibility for the spiritual lostness of the people who surround them (Eze. 3:18-19).

The dynamic is simple. If anyone, from any people group, is not part of God's kingdom they are considered lost, a mission field. On the other hand, if they profess to be a follower of Jesus Christ, they become part of the mission force.

 Missions should not become a formal program added later, as is typically the pattern. Rather, it should be a primary principle implanted at the moment a movement begins. In fact, any movement begins with this critical catalyst. Missions could be described as the heartbeat of a CPM.

Which concerns and critiques does this fruitful practice address? Most importantly, sound hermeneutics that emphasizes bringing closure to the Great Commission. Furthermore, as churches grow and multiply, locals contextualize the gospel when they evangelize their own. Finally, cross-cultural missions, not just evangelism, is also addressed when worldview transformation takes place (which is the third KRA).

> **SIDEBAR 6.1**
> ***EVANGELISM TOOL KIT***
> 1. Personal faith-story
> 2. C2C
> 3. Chronological Bible Storying
> 4. Firm Foundations

KRA/CSF #2: Reproduction/Generational

The primary characteristic of any movement is multiplication. This stands in stark contrast to planting churches by addition, i.e., planting one church at a time. Many mistakenly equate a movement with church addition.

The iconic verse of all movements is 2 Timothy 2:2. A close look at this passage notes that four generations pass on whatever they learn in the discipleship process. The CSF for reproduction is generational, therefore, growth to at least the fourth generation.

Reproduction provides feet to a movement. Experienced practitioners like George Patterson and Ying Kai stress not to invest time with individuals who fail to reproduce according to 2 Timothy 2:2. Rather, invest in those who obediently reproduce.

This KRA centers on the concerns and critiques that surrounds reproduction. It does not necessarily emphasize rapid reproduction, although the Wheel Model does not rule it out if all the other KRAs with corresponding CSFs are integrated.

KRA/CSF #3: Worldview Transformation/Obedience

The gospel must transform the very core of individuals, their families, and their societies. Without transformation, syncretism and/or legalism results. Scripture clearly states that God calls his followers to no longer conform to this world but to be transformed by the renewing of their minds (Rom. 12:2). Worldview transformation provides the needed Christ-centered impetus for a sustained movement. The Apostle Paul's ministry emphasized the same (Col. 1:28-29).

Essential to worldview transformation is the presentation of an accurate gospel so that people are born again and led by the Holy Spirit (Rom. 1:16; 1 Cor. 3:10-11). Laying a firm foundation through chronological Bible teaching is an effective method of teaching that can produce worldview transformation.

The CSF for gauging whether worldview transformation is taking place is obedience. For a sustained movement, the maturity level of all believers is based not on their knowledge of Scripture, but on whether they obey what they have learned (Matt. 28:20).

This KRA answers the more enduring question of sustainability, thus addressing issues related to worldview transformation. It also answers Steffen's critique related to genuineness of the movement. Western tendencies of expediency and pragmatism are also addressed here.

KRA/CSF #4: Ecclesiology/Self-Identification

In a CPM, one obvious assumption is that churches are being planted and multiplying. In the initial stages, the minimal biblical definition of church is typically applied (see Chapter 5).

The CSF for a group of believers to consider themselves a church is that they self-identify as representing the body of Christ in their area. Churches provide the skeletal structure of a movement so that the body of Christ can function in a healthy way, obeying the commands of Christ, including baptism and communion.

Each local church finds itself clothed with the culture in which it finds itself, thereby helping remove any sense of foreignness. Initially, new believers typically congregate in homes and are typically cellular in size. Smaller size churches reproduce more easily and rapidly. However, over time, the smaller cellular churches may grow larger or merge.

The Wheel Model explicitly addresses the core issue of planting churches with an ecclesiology that is grounded in Scripture.

KRA/CSF #5: Leadership/Outside Edge

For a movement to sustain itself, leadership development is essential. Leadership development provides the backbone of any movement.

But leadership development alone is not the CSF. The goal is to develop leadership out to the furthest edges of a movement. To ensure that competent leadership continues to emerge, various forms of follow-up training are practiced. Emerging leaders in a geographic area are often brought together at a convenient location for training. Once trained, they return to their homes to conduct the training of others on their own.

Itinerant leaders travel to those venues to assess, coach, and mentor the upcoming leaders. In some cases, itinerant trainers also have radio ministries to reinforce teaching. In addition, radio broadcasters respond to specific questions received by mail from the listening audience. In the era of cell phones, emerging leaders even in remote areas can call those mentoring them with specific questions. A good example of this integration is Far East Broadcasting Company's (FEBC) Hmong ministry.

Centrally-located Bible schools will not be able to provide this kind of leadership. In order to train leaders necessary to sustain a movement, lay leaders must be trained locally. In a sustained movement, leadership is developed alongside the multiplication of churches. In fact, the discipleship of leaders is integrated within the movement itself as leaders obey what they are being taught evidenced through the multiplication of churches and the mentoring of other leaders. Formal, or even nonformal theological training, does not set the standard for leadership selection.

Critics pointed to leadership development as an area of concern. The Wheel Model not only addresses this aspect of a movement but also stresses the arena where leadership development should focus, the outer edges of a movement.

A movement ceases to exist if leadership reproduction fails to reach the outside edges of a movement. Emerging churches will not survive long term if leaders are not trained to disciple, shepherd new believers, and handle emerging pastoral concerns, such as, births, weddings, sickness, funerals.

Critics were also concerned about discipleship. When analyzing the data, I realized that discipleship was a subset of training. Training covered all aspects related to the discipleship of leaders and local believers. Current movements evidence consistent and focused training. Some movements, like the T4T model, are actually described as "discipleship movements."

Using a living organism analogy, Table 8 summarizes the fruitful practices and their relevance towards a sustained movement.

TABLE 8
A SUSTAINED MOVEMENT:
A LIVING ORGANISM ANALOGY

Fruitful Practices for a Sustained Movement	Organism Analogy
Mission	Heart
Reproduction	Feet
Leadership	Backbone
Ecclesiology	Skeleton
Worldview transformation	Brain/mind

THE RIM

The rim of a wheel holds the spokes and hub in place. In this model, four important elements feed back into the spokes. This is in contrast to the hub that energizes the spokes outwardly. Because they are critical to the success of *each* of the fruitful practices, I labeled the rim elements universals.

Four important universals emerged throughout the research. Although they did not emerge as singular themes, they were scattered throughout the dominant themes, i.e., fruitful practices. The four universals include: modeling, prayer, indigenization, and training.

Surprisingly in the research, the role of the missionary was ubiquitous. The modeling of the outsider was a critical factor in all aspects of a sustained movement. The missionary's attitude, gifting, training, modeling, and vision, helped encourage or destroy a movement. While all participants agreed that birthing a movement was in the hands of a sovereign God, they also agreed that the potential of a movement was in the hands of the missionary.

As described above, the role of the missionary, primarily through modeling, plays a critical role in a sustained movement. In other words, the outsider must model each of the Fruitful Practices.

In addition to modeling from the outsider, three other Universals must also be integrated into the five Fruitful Practices. For example, consider how indigenization influences each of the spokes. Indigenization emphasizes that it is local missions, local leadership, local reproduction, local ecclesiology, and local worldview transformation (see: Table 9).

TABLE 9
INDIGENIZATION FACTORS INTEGRATED THROUGHOUT EACH FRUITFUL PRACTICE

Fruitful Practices	Indigenization Factor Integrated Into Fruitful Practices
Mission	Local believers feel responsible for taking the gospel to their own people as well as other people groups (Rom. 1:16)
Leadership	Local believers take responsibility for leading at all levels (Col. 3:23)
Reproduction	Local believers, leaders, and churches are reproducing (Acts 6:7)
Ecclesiology	Church is conducted contextually (Acts 15:19)
Worldview Transformation	Biblical transformation takes place among the local believers as local worldview issues are addressed biblically (Rom. 12:2)

Prayer is a vital part of all aspects of the ministry. It is how the practitioner connects God with the movement, or perhaps more accurately, *how God connects the practitioner with the movement.* Jesus said in John 14:13-14, "And I will do whatever you ask in my name, so that the Son may bring glory to the Father. You may ask me for anything in my name, and I will do it." Even though prayer may not be *the* work, without it the practitioner has *no* work (see Table 10).

TABLE 10
PRAYER INTEGRATED THROUGHOUT EACH FRUITFUL PRACTICE

Fruitful Practices	Prayer Integrated into Fruitful Practices
Mission	Prayer energizes the mission as believers connect with God's missional heart (Luke 22:42)
Leadership	Through prayer, leaders are raised up and chosen. A key characteristic of a leader is his consistent prayer life (Acts 13:2-3)
Reproduction	Through prayer God gives the growth of a movement (2 Thess. 3:1)
Ecclesiology	God commands his people to pray. Prayer is a key characteristic of a thriving church (Acts 2:42)
Worldview Transformation	Believers are transformed as they cultivate an intimacy with Christ through prayer (Prov. 15:29; Phil. 4:6-7; Heb. 4:16; 1 Pet. 3:12)

Appropriate, biblically-based training that is often informal, is inherent throughout the Wheel Model. Characteristic of all training within a sustainable movement is that it is obedience-based rather than knowledge-based. This would be true whether the training is delivered through a literate, semi-literate, or an oral approach (see Table 11).

TABLE 11
PRAYER INTEGRATED THROUGHOUT EACH FRUITFUL PRACTICE

Fruitful Practices	Training Integrated into Fruitful Practices
Mission	Every believer has been trained to share his faith. The effect of the training is measured by whether or not believers are obediently evangelizing. (Phlm. 6)
Leadership	Constant, relevant training is essential for development and multiplication of leadership (1 Tim. 4:16)
Reproduction	Leaders and believers are trained to reproduce what they have learned (2 Tim.2:2)
Ecclesiology	Followers have been trained to obey the seven commands of Christ14 (Matt. 28:20), or simply the Great Commission and the Great Commandment
Worldview Transformation	Worldview is transformed as believers learn to obey (John 8:31)

NOW WHERE?

It is now time to compare and contrast the Wheel Model with Garrison's 10 Universals and 10 Common Factors, along with the CPM concerns and criticisms. Garrison will comment on some of the critiques.

The WHEEL MODEL

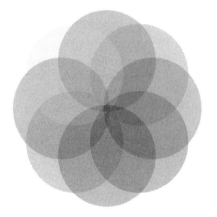

CHAPTER 7

THE WHEEL MODEL vs. CPMS & THE CRITICS

How well does the Wheel Model compare with Garrison's 10 Universals and 10 Common Factors? How well does it address the concerns and criticisms of critics? This chapter will attempt to answer these questions, again categorizing them under the four legs of missiology: missions history, social sciences, theology, and strategy. But one caveat will be added. For the sake of integrity, I asked Garrison to make his own assessments as well.[1] His observations will be found in bold lettering under the Critiques section in the tables below. I begin with Garrison's 10 universals.

CONTRASTING GARRISON'S 10 UNIVERSALS WITH THE WHEEL MODEL

Garrison described 10 universals that he believes characterize all CPMs: (1) prayer, (2) abundant gospel sowing, (3) intentional church planting, (4) authority of Scripture,

(5) local leadership, (6) lay leadership, (7) cell or house churches, (8) churches planting churches, (9) rapid reproduction, and (10) healthy churches.[2] Table 12 compares the Wheel Model with Garrison's 10 Universals showing similarities and differences.

TABLE 12
COMPARING THE 10 UNIVERSALS WITH THE 11 MINISTRY PRACTICES OF THE WHEEL MODEL

Sustainability Wheel Model	10 Universals
Role of the Holy Spirit	No
Vision	No
Mission (lostness)	Implied
Leadership (outside edge)	Yes
Church ecclesiology (self-identification)	Implied
Worldview transformation (obedience)	Implied
Reproduction (generational)	Yes
Prayer	Yes
Indigenous	Yes
Training	No
Role of the missionary	No

Are the differences that emerged in Table 12 significant? They appear to be for the following reasons. Garrison has always maintained that his definition and the 10 Universals are descriptive, not prescriptive.[3] While the Wheel Model is also descriptive, as many nuances of church planting are not included, it does provide practitioners a visual template to observe two important observations. First, it shows the integration of fruitful practices, unlike the 10 Universals. Secondly, it provides a visual template that helps the practitioner (and evaluators) assess current church planting activities to assure the coverage and integration of all the key areas.

Typically, lists are not easy to remember because many people are visual learners. Having a visual model, therefore, helps make the multiple concepts easier to grasp.

Additionally, the Wheel Model emphasizes the themes necessary for a sustained movement that are absent in Garrison's 10 Universals. These include: (1) the role of the Holy Spirit, (2) vision, (3) training, and (4) the important role of modeling.

The Wheel Model also makes explicit those themes that are implicit in Garrison's 10 Universals. These include: (1) mission, (2) ecclesiology, and (3) worldview transformation.

Garrison's 10 Universals, while limited, remain helpful. I have used them to evaluate a team's ministry activities, and will continue to do so because it keeps teams focused on the universal elements inherent to all CPMs. In addition, because many trained in CPM principles already have Garrison's 10 Universals as a conceptual framework, it remains important to continue helping them assess their movement from a familiar framework.

In comparison, the Wheel Model describes a sustainable movement more precisely and contributes to the current discussion about CPMs. But more importantly, it provides the necessary conceptual framework for teams to organize their priorities during the launch and planning phases of engaging a people group by addressing and answering the fundamental, missiological questions central to a sustainable movement.

WHEEL MODEL VERSUS CPM CONCERNS AND CRITICISMS

I will now evaluate Garrisons's 10 Common Factors,[4] noting if the critics' concerns and criticisms leveled at CPMs are addressed by the Wheel Model. Tables 13 through 16 summarize the contrasts following the four legs of missiology: missions history, social sciences, theology, and strategy. Garrison will comment on some of the questions (see bolded). I will then draw some conclusions for the future.

TABLE 13
ASSESSMENT OF CONCERNS AND CRITICISMS RELATED TO MISSIONS HISTORY

Critiques	Wheel Model	CPM
Does the biblical record, particularly Acts, provide evidence of movements that were rapid, incorporating large numbers of new converts?	Yes	Yes
Is speedy multiplication consistent with Pauline teams?	No, but OK if happens	Yes
Is there historical evidence of movements outside of Scripture? Were they considered good?	Yes	Yes
Does history show that movements are a natural feature for people groups entering Christianity?	Yes	Yes

TABLE 14
ASSESSMENT OF CONCERNS AND CRITICISMS RELATED TO THE SOCIAL SCIENCES

Critiques	Wheel Model	CPM
Why is incarnation downplayed? (**"Actually, it would be more accurate to say that 'foreign' incarnational ministry is not emphasized."**)	Yes	No
Does linguistics for expatriates have a role in movements? (**"This question presupposes that expatriates are the driving force of what is happening."**)	Yes	No
What role should language and culture acquisition play for expatriates? (**"I doubt that any mission agency has stronger language-acquisition requirements than the IMB – however, it is right to say that the heavy emphasis on nationals and an indigenous movement makes the expat's language acquisition less vital than in a foreigner-dependent paradigm."**)	Yes	No
What is the role for contextualization? (**"Contextualization is a foreign concern that is eclipsed by the heavy emphasis on indigenization."**)	Yes	Unclear
How indigenous are the churches? (**"There is something of an oxymoron in this question. For Westerners to establish an indigenous church is an oxymoron. In CPMs one emphasizes 'obedience to all things Christ has commanded,' and then allows indigenous forms to emerge."**)	Yes	No

The WHEEL MODEL

What indigenous symbols and rituals will require Christian substitutes?	Yes	No
How well do expatriates understand the economic system so that dependency does not result? (**"CPMs are all about avoiding and breaking the bonds of dependency by stimulating indigenous, not foreign-dependent, movements of evangelism and church multiplication."**)	Yes	No
How well do expatriates understand the social system so that they know how Christianity will spread?	Yes	Somewhat
How well do expatriates understand the political system so that they know what governance looks like on multiple levels?	Yes	No
How well do expatriates understand the host culture's pedagogical preferences so that they can communicate effectively? (**"This question presupposes that expatriates are the driving force of what is happening. That is an unfortunate 'old paradigm' misunderstanding."**)	Yes	No
How well so expatriates understand the local worldview so that they can identify bridges and barriers for initial evangelism?	Yes	No
How well do expatriates understand the local worldview so that worldview transformation is maximized? (**"This question presupposes that expatriates are the driving force of what is happening. That is an unfortunate 'old paradigm' misunderstanding."**)	Yes	No

TABLE 15
ASSESSMENT OF CONCERNS AND CRITICISMS RELATED TO THEOLOGY

Critiques	Wheel Model	CPM
Does Scripture support large numbers of people converting to Christianity within a short time period?	Yes	Assumed
Does the definition of church meet biblical standards? (**"Yes. Of course, there is no single definition of the church in the Bible. Instead, CPMs seek to approximate the Acts 1:1 dictate that the church would 'continue the life and teachings of Jesus'. The foundation for this is structuring church around 'obey(ing) all things whatsoever I have commanded you'** (Matt. 28:20).")	Yes	Unclear
Is the role of ecclesiology emphasized in sustaining a movement? (**"Increasingly it is. CPMers are realizing that at the heart of every CPM is 'C', i.e. a church."**)	Yes	Unclear
What is the role of ecclesiology in sustaining a movement?	Yes	Yes
How Western is their ecclesiology?	Yes	Yes
How well do they understand hermeneutics?	Yes	Yes
How much social transformation takes place within society? (**"This begins with locating and engaging the person of peace who is the first evidence that the Holy Spirit is already at work. A CPM watchword has often been: 'Find where God is at work and join Him.'"**)	Yes	Unclear

How much foundation for the gospel is laid? ("This occurs post-conversion through obedience-based discipleship.")	Yes	Unclear
Does an accurate gospel challenge each generation's worldview through bridges and barriers?	Yes	Unclear
How well does each generation capture the metanarrative of Scripture?	Yes	Unclear
If Scripture is unavailable, how is it provided? Is translation part of the strategy? (Yes, but stemming from an indigenous momentum, rather than an exogenous impulse.")	No	No
Have reciprocates captured missions or just evangelism?	Yes	Yes
Is the gospel presented focusing on honor-shame rather than guilt-innocence, as is typical in the West? ("Because CPMs so quickly become indigenous, this 'foreign issue' is less of an issue.")	No	No
What theological curricula are planned? Who develops it? Disperses it?	Yes	Yes
How are signs and wonders handled when one's theology does not address them? ("As the situation dictates the spirit world is engaged, but not as a strategy of advance or initiation.")	Unclear	Unclear
Does the discipleship phase have adequate depth to sustain a movement for four generations?	Yes	Yes

How are symbols, rituals, phases of life contextualized so that Christianity becomes a total way of life?	Unclear	Unclear
Has each generation of the movement avoided extensive syncretism?	Unclear	Unclear
Does regeneration accompany each generation?	Unclear	Unclear
Who trains potential leadership in each generation?	Unclear	Unclear
What is the role of Bible schools?	Unclear	Unclear

TABLE 16
ASSESSMENT OF CONCERNS AND CRITICISMS RELATED TO STRATEGY

Critiques	Wheel Model	CPM
Are CPMs driven by foreign funds, thereby unsustainable long-term? How reproducible is the expatriate model?	Yes	Yes
Who models the various phases of church planting to the locals? How much? By whom?	Yes	Yes
Are indigenous pedagogical styles used by expatriates? Locals? (**"Actually, as we model and teach our national partners to conduct 'participative' Bible study in weekly worship, we are modeling a 'style' of pedagogy that allows for maximum discipleship and self-correcting dynamics."**)	Yes	No

How is leadership developed?	Yes	Yes
Does an exit strategy drive the expatriate?	Yes	Yes
Should holistic ministry have a role? (**"See my "Handy Guide for Healthy Churches" on the CPMs.com website for more insight on this topic. By structuring church around the five purposes of worship, fellowship, ministry, discipleship, and evangelism/missions holistic ministry indigenously emerges.** **In the Handy Guide, we advocate structuring everything the church does around the 'Great Commandment' and the 'Great Commission' from which we get the 5 purposes of a church. These 5 purposes emulate the life and ministry of Christ, ensure that the church is biblically sound, and assure a holistic indigenous expression of Christ and His gospel in the community."**)	No	No
How much do American Western values, such as expediency and pragmatism, drive CPMs? (**"The highly indigenous nature of CPMs render this a non-issue."**)	Yes	No
What role does ethnodoxology (worship songs / ordinances / lifecycle and calendric rituals / Bible translation, etc.) play?	Yes	Some
What role do partnerships play so that a comprehensive Christianity is offered?	No	No
How do locals representing generations 2-4 view CPMs?	Yes	Yes

SUMMARIZING THE CONTRAST

The above tables addressed the CPM concerns and criticisms in relationship to the Wheel Model. What are the major conclusions that emerged? First, as already noted in previous chapters, CPMs are highly focused on reproduction and multiplication. In some instances, this is the most significant contribution that CPM methodology has made to church growth. However, because of such a strong emphasis on rapid multiplication, anthropological concerns seem to be left unaddressed, particularly those related to worldview.

Second, during discussions with Garrison he recognized that CPM practitioners must do a much better job of addressing ecclesiological concerns. His conviction is that ecclesiology is the number one factor necessary for a sustained movement. Table 15 supports that claim.

A third result that emerged from these comparisons is that neither the Wheel Model nor CPM emphasized holistic ministry. Although the analysis of holistic ministry is outside the specific scope of this research project, it merits further study.

A fourth area of concern that is absent in both the Wheel Model and Garrison's 10 Universals is Bible translation. CPM practitioners often raise this issue, particularly those working among minority groups that are illiterate and without Scripture in their language. Some question if it is even being responsible to begin evangelism and church planting among illiterate groups without it. In light of these questions, it is important to make a comment here.

Though my research and this book does not address Bible translation specifically, many within the Jonathan Project network do not believe that illiteracy should be a barrier for people to receive the gospel, and then be discipled into a movement. A very good example is Taikadai's work with the Kaobu. This movement, as explained in the opening chapter, is based entirely on oral approaches of presenting a meta-narrative of the gospel. The movement continues to grow both mono-culturally and cross-culturally despite severe persecution by relatives and communist authorities.

Taikadai and his team of local trainers/missionaries currently train numerous other teams in these same approaches. Other teams, once trained in oral approaches, are seeing similar results, though all are still very much in the early stages of a potential movement.

Though these are all exciting developments, other serious questions emerge as a result. For example, as the gospel crosses from one language group to another, what terminology is used for God, Satan, sin, hell, salvation, etc. Are the terms borrowed? Are local believers that witness cross-culturally aware of the potential linguistic risks that come when the gospel crosses cultures? Taikadai helps us here as he tells his experience.

> *The teams we have trained all have both expats and locals involved. We expect that all the M's have had enough training to be aware of the importance of word choice. In fact we*

> know they do. It has been my experience that the locals are more inclined to borrow from the national language or religious language without the concerns and questions that a good missionary would bring to the task. If a missionary isn't aware of the issues when pioneering translations then may God have mercy! We also believe it is the role of the locals for contextualization, not the outsider, although the questions most likely need to be asked by the outsider. My role with our team was to ask questions about terminology, to encourage research into Buddhism, Christians who were Buddhists, monks, etc., and to urge the process of challenging existing words used from the high religion and language. It was a short time before they saw improved communication and changed their long-standing approaches.[5]

Taikadai and his team use an oral Bible with new believers, integrating it with CPM methodology, mass-communication, i.e., radio, and chronological redemptive teaching that stresses the meta-narrative of Scripture. Taikadai and his team offer these insights that other pioneer workers may find helpful.

> If you are referring to the idea of an oral Bible that is static and highly detailed versus Bible storying that may reflect the tellers ability

or the hearer's context, then I am aware of the difference. I believe David Watson has published an article about this. We have as our goal an oral Bible in the heart of the believers that they can carry with them wherever they go and that insights and revelation is available from the knowledge of the story and the work of the Living Holy Spirit in them. We have numerous examples of this happening. I do not stand with some groups that want people to memorize and communicate orally the literate format in the Bible of a story. I believe in story crafting, simplify to multiply and the knowledge that God will bring a desire to read to a redeemed people eventually.[6]

So what role does Bible translation have in a sustained movement? A critical one as ultimately the believers should learn to read the entire Bible on their own and in their own language as a way of self-feeding. Self-feeding is a critical aspect in sustaining a movement and establishing healthy churches. But ultimately, does self-feeding demand literacy? The Kaobu team with Taikadai take the following approach.

The Kaobu groups we have worked with have a Bible, although a poorly translated one, but the sub-groups we work with are illiterate. Do we encourage literacy? Yes. There are now 20 or more Kaobu in Laos who can read

Kaobu. We did not believe it was our main task to provide literacy but have developed a short primer that has been used locally. We found most didn't want to learn to read at first.

In opposition to the high view of literacy, every cult I have encountered whether in the USA, Burma, China or Laos, has used the Bible to deceive. The latest is a Hmong 7th day Adventist twisting Scripture and preying upon real believers who are susceptible in Thailand and Laos. Those who read poorly and have not been brought up in an environment that really encourages intimacy with the living Christ through fellowship and the emphasis on obedience versus knowledge-based education are most prone to be led astray by savvy Bible teachers. The guys we have trained have consistently resisted cults or religious leaders who want to exert control over them in return for finances, but not all will stand. We have had some turn to the dark side for financial reasons.

Because there are daily radio broadcasts, many have tapes, CD's, SD cards and know praise and worship songs I believe the people are able to self-feed from these tools. I don't see many Kaobu people even in Thailand where they almost all can read Kaobu spending

> time reading. They are not a book culture. So to answer the question does self-feeding demand literacy? I believe not, just as in the early church most people were not literate yet they grew in their understanding and faith by listening to others teaching and also through getting to know God in prayer and through the stories they heard or experienced themselves.[7]

Currently our team is targeting an unreached group of Hmong in China. We have recruited local farmers of one Hmong dialect to be the missionary evangelists to this new unreached group of Hmong. In the process of assembling a team of cross-cultural workers, career Bible translators were recruited to work simultaneously with the church planting effort. So while evangelism and church planting take place based on oral methods, Bible translators determine key terms, working out a script, recruiting and training local translators, and translating key portions of Scripture for teaching the gospel meta-narrative. I believe this is the best way to launch a pioneering effort among illiterate unreached people groups.

Finally, the Wheel Model incorporates other important factors necessary for a sustained movement, i.e., what has been learned through the CGM and CPMs.

DEFINING A SUSTAINABLE MOVEMENT

In Chapter 5, I suggested using a replacement acronym for CPM. Why? Because the phrase Church Planting Movement raises too many questions in the minds of critics, both founded and unfounded. By using a more accurate term along with a more descriptive/prescriptive model, critics might be more convinced to accept CPMs as a viable church planting option for the complete evangelization of a people group.

In addition, it would encourage practitioners to press on and would provide another lens through which they can plan, implement, and assess their current church planting efforts.

What should that phrase be? In light of the research and resulting grounded theory model, the Jonathan Project ministry promotes the phrase Sustainable Church Multiplication Movements (S-CMMs). Although the Wheel Model is more helpful than a definition, I will also add a definition to the mix. In an S-CMM, God enables Spirit-transformed disciples to form biblically grounded and indigenous churches multiplying rapidly to at least the fourth generation, with trained local leadership, reaching out cross-culturally.

HOW UNIVERSAL IS THE MODEL?

Since the geographical limitation of this study is East Asia, one might assume that the model is limited to that context. However, the participants of this study came from a variety of church planting environments within East Asia, from urban to very rural, and from conglomerate secularized urban environments to tightly knit social family networks found among tribal people of various religions.

In addition, a number of the research participants coach numerous movements outside of East Asia. In fact, the participants within this study have a working knowledge from a conglomerate of movements around the globe numbering over 640. In light of this, the Wheel Model may have potential transferability to other church planting environments worldwide, although changes in praxis may be warranted.

CONCLUSION

In conclusion, I will emphasize two things. First, if one's goal is to see the complete evangelization of people groups around the world, then S-CMM principles must be taken seriously. Second, for those engaged in CPM methodology, best practices that contribute to a sustained movement, both short and long term, should be integrated into one's ministry. The Wheel Model highlights the key elements of a sustained church multiplication movement.

DEFINITIONS

10/40 Window - A term coined by Luis Bush, a mission strategist, referring to those regions of the eastern hemisphere, plus the European and African part of the Western hemisphere, located between 10 and 40 degrees north of the equator, a general area that in 1990 was purported to have the highest level of socioeconomic challenges, the major religions of the world, and the least access to the Christian message and Christian resources on the planet.

Church - A group of born again Christ disciples that self identify as a local community of believers representing Christ to those around them, carrying out the three-fold ministry of worship, ministering the Word and spiritual gifts within the body, and fulfilling the Great Commission.

Church Growth Movement (CGM) - The emphasis on church growth as the natural expression of a healthy church. Donald McGavran was the father of this movement. Other strong proponents included Charles Kraft, Allan Tippett, Ralph Winter, and C. P. Wagner.

Church Multiplication Movement (CMM) - A God-caused, locally led expansion of the church in which churches plant churches, leaders raise up leaders, and trainers equip trainers. A people group experiencing a CMM usually reaches out in mission to another people group (e.g., JT, Philippines).[1]

Church Planting Movement (CPM) - "A rapid multiplication of indigenous churches planting churches that sweeps though a people group or population segment."[2] Generational reproduction out to at least the fourth generation of churches, leaders, and believers is a key assumption of a CPM.

Holistic Ministry - A method of addressing both physical and spiritual needs of people. Within the context of CPMs, it is "Promoting transformational training that helps produce new communities of worshippers capable of reproducing themselves. There's ongoing discipleship, and there's ongoing social transformation."[3]

Ecclesiology - "Ecclesiology is a discipline that undertakes critical and constructive reflection on the Christian community as a distinct social body in the world and as a particular people in history." [4]

Indigenous Biblical Church Movement (IBCM) - A gospel-generated CPM, using local resources with the goal of worldview and societal transformation, resulting in a church on mission.

> **Communication of the Gospel** - Heavy focus on communicating the redemptive story through chronological Bible teaching, narrative, and orality (Luke 24:27, 44; 1 Cor. 3:10).
>
> **CPM** - A serious commitment to church planting as the primary strategy for reaching a people group where every local church (congregation) plants other churches (Eph. 3:10), where every leader is mentoring other leaders (2 Tim. 2:2), and where speed and multi-generational growth beyond the third generation are key factors in measuring success (2 Thess. 3:1).
>
> **Local Resources** - High commitment to immediate indigenization, contextualization, and reproducibility, resulting in very little foreign funding being used to spark or sustain a movement by paying local evangelists and pastors (2 Cor. 8:2-4). No outside funding should be used to pay local people ministers; this practice by usually well-meaning people is the greatest hurdle to CPMs.

Worldview and Societal Transformation - An unshakable belief in the transforming power of the Word of God and the Holy Spirit to transform individual lives and entire people groups (Rom. 1:16, 12:1).

Mission - A deep commitment to join God in His mission to reach every people group (Matt. 24:14, 28:18-20).[5]

Jonathan Project (JP) - Identifies, mobilizes, trains, and coaches Jonathans, those individuals capable of facilitating IBCMs among least-reached people groups.

Jonathan Training (JT) - Trains, inspires, and coaches Jonathan types for effective IBCM ministry.

Mass Movement - An entire tribe or caste converts en masse to Christianity. This phrase was first coined by J. W. Pickett (1890-1981) while a missionary in India. Early missiologists thought the term was too vague so it was replaced by the term People Movement.

People Movement (PM) - The joint decision of a number of individuals, all from the same people group, that enables them to become Christians without social dislocation. They remain in full contact with their non-Christian relatives, thus enabling other segments of that people group, across the years and after suitable instruction, to come to similar decisions and form Christian churches made up exclusively of members of that group.[6]

Strategy Coordinator (SC) - One who develops or implements a strategy to reach a people group, working with a team or network.[7]

Strategy Coordinator Training - The IMB's CPM training.

Sustainability - "Governed or maintained by, or produced as a result of, such practices."[8] In the context of church movements it pertains to entropy affecting a CPM and the ongoing, total health of the churches through worldview transformation of soul and body.

Ten Common Factors - Characteristics that Garrison identified as being common to CPMs but not part of the 10 Universals that are a part of every CPM.[9]

Training for Trainers (T4T) - An application of CPM principles pioneered by Ying Kai of the IMB where the focus is on training other trainers who will train others to do church planting, currently one of the most effective ways to facilitate a CPM.[10]

Worldview - "A set of presuppositions (assumptions that may be true, partially true, or entirely false) that we hold (consciously or subconsciously, consistently or inconsistently) about the makeup of the world."[11]

NOTES

Chapter 1
1. All scripture citations are taken from the NIV.
2. Garrison, 1999, p. 6.
3. Garrison, 1999, p. 7.
4. Smith & Kai, 2011, p. 21.
5. A. Smith, personal communication, December 5, 2008. See Hobbs' *Dawn Harvest* and *Dawn Reepers* for the inside story.
6. C. Sergeant, personal communication, 1998.
7. C. Sergeant, personal communication, July 14, 1998.
8. Taikadai, personal communication, December 3, 2011, April 15, 2013.
9. Bishop, 2010.
10. Steffen, 2011, p. 355.
11. Mark, 2011a, ¶9.
12. Sills, 2010, pp. 170-171.
13. Steffen, 2011, p. 355.
14. Myers, 1999, p. 234.
15. Steffen, 1997, pp. 133-134.
16. Hmong Shaman, personal communication, 1996.
17. Mallow, 1998, p. 25.
18. T. S. Hum, personal communication, 2012.
19. Steffen, 2011, p. 166.
20. C. Dillon, personal communication, November 23, 2012.
21. Ott and Wilson, 2011, p. 79.
22. J. D. Payne, personal communication, July 2, 2012.
23. Hodge, 1953, p. 15.

Chapter 2
1. Harnack, 1961, pp. 1,15.
2. McIntosh, 2012, p. 197.
3. Fletcher, 1999, p. 85.
4. Fletcher, 1999, p. 86.
5. Hillgarth, 1986, pp. 168, 170, 174.
6. Neill, 1965, p. 74.
7. Carver, 2003, p. 15.
8. Neill, 1965, pp. 74, 77, 78.
9. Winter, 1999, pp. 263-266; 2009, p. 265.

[10] Nevius, 1886, pp. Preface, 8, 10, 42-44.
[11] Nevius, 1866, p. 58.
[12] Nevius, 1866, p. 43.
[13] Nevius, 1866, p. 66.
[14] Nevius, 1866, p. 83.
[15] Warnack, 1954, p. 198.
[16] Warnack, 1954, pp. 224-248.
[17] Warnack, 1954, p. 19.
[18] Keysser, 1980, p. 24.
[19] Keysser, 1980, p. xvii.
[20] Keysser, 1980, pp. xiv, 57.
[21] Keysser, 1980, p. ix.
[22] Keysser, 1980, p. 12.
[23] Keysser, 1980, p. 13.
[24] Keysser, 1980, p. 26.
[25] Payne, 2012, pp. 12, 18.
[26] Allen, 1929, p. 7.
[27] Allen, 1964a, p. vii.

Chapter 3
[1] McPhee, 2002, pp. 31-32.
[2] Pickett, Warnshius, Singh, & McGavran, 1956, p. ix.
[3] Kraft, 2005, p. 22.
[4] Keysser, 1980, pp. x-xii.
[5] McIntosh, 2012, p. 184.
[6] Parsons, 2012, p. 163.
[7] Middleton, 1990, p. 129.
[8] McPhee, 2001, p. 443.
[9] McGavran, 2005, p. 91.
[10] Parsons, 2012, p. 165.
[11] McGavran and Wagner, 1990, p. 163.
[12] Wodarz, 1979, p. 185.
[13] Parsons, 2012, p. 170.
[14] McGavran, 1955a, p. v; 1955b, p. 24.
[15] McGavran, 1955b, p. 81; 1970, p. 298.
[16] McGavran, 1955a, p. 4; 1984, p. 124.
[17] McGavran, 1970, p. 49, 51, 63, 265, 275, 285, 338, 347.
[18] McGavran, 1972, p. 79.
[19] Tippett, 1987, p. 75.
[20] Tippett, 1973b, pp. 123-124.
[21] Takamizawa, 1977, p. 219.
[22] Tippett, 1967, p. 30; 1970, pp. 19, 50; 1987, p. xxiii.
[23] Tippett, 1973a, p. 128; 1973b, p. 149.
[24] McGavran, 1972, p. 79.
[25] Winter, 1974, pp. 226-241.
[26] Kraft, 2005, p. 90.

[27] Kraft, 2005, p. 97.
[28] G. Parsons, personal communication, October 29, 2012.
[29] Kraft, 2005, p. 110.
[30] Kraft, 2005, p. 114.
[31] Kraft, 2005, p. 115.
[32] See: C. Douglas McConnell, ed., The Holy Spirit and Mission Dynamics, 1997.
[33] Garrison, 1999, p. 33.
[34] D. Garrison, personal communication, December 19, 2012.
[35] Garrison, 2004, p. 24.
[36] D. Garrison, personal communication, September 29, 2012.
[37] V. Middleton, personal communication, September 2012.
[38] G. McIntosh, personal communication, November 29, 2012.
[39] V. Middleton, personal communication, September 2012.
[40] D. Garrison, personal communication, September 29, 2012.
[41] Garrison, 2004, p. 28.
[42] Garrison, 2004, p. 26.
[43] Garrison, 2004, p. 303.

Chapter 4
[1] Winter, 2009, p. 265; 1999, p. 263-266.
[2] See: Steffen, "Chronological practices and possibilities in the urban world." *Global Missiology*. 2013, 4(10). <http://ojs.globalmissiology.org/index.php/english/issue/view/107>
[3] McIlwain, 1987, pp. 7-8.
[4] Steffen, 1994, p. 366.
[5] Sheffield, 1990.
[6] McIlwain 1987; Steffen 1994, pp. 365-366.
[7] Garrison, 1999; 2004.
[8] Keane, 2007, p. 37.
[9] Keane, 2007, p. 43.
[10] Steffen, 2011, pp. 31-32.
[11] Steffen, 2011, p. xiii.
[12] Smith and Kai, 2011, p. 189.

Chapter 5
[1] Taber, 2000:10.
[2] Neely, 2000:633.
[3] Tippett 1987:xiii.
[4] Irenaeus Tertullian, *Tertullian's Plea for Allegiance A.2*, AD 197, cited in Smith & Kai, 2011, p. 32.
[5] Pliny cited in Smith & Kai, 2011, p. 31.
[6] C. Sergeant, personal communication, Jan. 3, 2014.
[7] J.D. Payne, personal communication: Dec. 17, 2013.
[8] C. Sergeant, personal communication, Jan. 3, 2014.
[9] J.D. Payne, personal communication, Dec. 14, 2013.
[10] J.D. Payne, personal communication, Feb. 3, 2014.

[11] Stone, Introduction, n.p.
[12] J.D. Payne, personal communication, Dec. 14, 2013.
[13] D. Garrison, personal communication, Dec. 14, 2013.
[14] Steffen, 1997, p. 134.
[15] Ott and Wilson, 2011, p. 79.
[16] Steffen, 2011, p. 132.
[17] C. Sergeant, personal communication, March 2, 2013.
[19] Steffen, 2011, p. 355.
[20] T. Steffen, personal communication, January 3, 2013.
[21] Steffen, 2011, p. 355.

Chapter 6
[1] Calvin, 2009, ¶ 2.
[2] Taylor, 1998, p. 227.
[3] Taylor, 1998, p. 228.
[4] Grist, 1916, p. 179.
[5] Grist, 1916, p. 180.

Chapter 7
[1] Personal communication, Jan. 1, 2013.
[2] Garrison, 1999, pp. 33-36.
[3] Garrison, 1999, pp. 3, 6, 42-43; 2004, p. 21.
[4] Garrison, 1999, pp. 3, 6, 42-43; 2004, p. 21.
[5] Taikadai, personal communication, Jan. 25, 2014.
[6] Taikadai, personal communication, Jan. 25, 2014.
[7] Kaobu team with Taikadai, personal communication, Jan. 25, 2014.

Definitions
[1] A. Smith, Personal communication, 2004.
[2] Garrison, 2004, p. 21.
[3] Steffen, 2011, p. 347.
[4] Stone, Introduction, n.p.
[5] International Jonathan Project Executive Committee, 2011.
[6] Wagner, 1990, p. 223.
[7] The Traveling Team, 2013, ¶ 40.
[8] Agnes, 2000, p. 1443.
[9] Garrison, 1999.
[10] Smith & Kai, 2011, p. 36.
[11] Sire, 2004, p. 19.

REFERENCES

AD2000 & beyond movement. (1999). Retrieved from http://www.ad2000.org/ad2kbroc.htm

Agnes, M. (Ed.). (2000). *Webster's New World College Dictionary (4th ed.)*. Foster City, CA: IDG Books Worldwide.

Allen, R. (1929). *The spontaneous expansion of the church*. London, England: World Dominion Press.

Allen, R. (1962). *The spontaneous expansion of the church*. Grand Rapids, MI: Eerdmans.

Allen, R. (1964a). *Missionary methods: St. Paul's or ours*. Grand Rapids, MI: Eerdmans.

Allen, R. (1964b). *Missionary principles*. Grand Rapids, MI: Eerdmans.

Birkey, D. (1991, January). The house church: A missiological model. *Missiology: An International Review, 19*(1), 69-80.

Bishop, P. (2010, February 2). Jonathan training [Powerpoint case study]. Training meeting conducted at OMF Mission Home, Phnom Penh, Cambodia.

Brawner, J. (2007, Spring). An examination of nine key issues concerning CPM. *Journal of Evangelism and Missions, 6*, 3-13.

Calvin, J. (2009). *Commentary on Zechariah, Malachi*. Retrieved from http://www.ccel.org/ccel/calvin/calcom30

Carey, W. (1999). An enquiry into the obligations of Christians to use means for the conversion of the heathens. In R. D. Winter, S. C. Hawthorne, D. R. Dorr, D. B. Graham, B. A. Koch (Eds.), *Perspectives on the world Christian movement: A reader* (3rd ed.) (pp. 293–299). Pasadena, CA: William Carey Library.

Carver, M. E. (Ed.). (2003). *The cross goes north: Process of conversion in northern Europe AD 300–1300*. Suffolk, United Kingdom: York Medieval Press.

Cho, Y. (2010, July-August). Challenge and opportunity for the global network of mission structures. *Mission Frontiers*. Retrieved from http://www.missionfrontiers.org/issue/article/challenge-and-opportunity-for-the-global-network-of-mission-structures

Culbertson, H. (2012, September 27). 10/40 Window: Do you need to be stirred to action? [Website]. Retrieved from http://home.snu.edu/~hculbert/1040.htm

Discipling a whole nation. (2001). A report on the state of evangelical churches in the Philippines 2000. Unpublished report. Discipling a Whole Nation organization.

Escobar, S. (2002). *Changing tides: Latin America and mission today*. Maryknoll, NY: Orbis Books.

Fletcher, R. (1999). *The barbarian conversion: From paganism to Christianity*. New York, NY: H. Holt.
Garrison, D. (1999). *Church planting movements*. Richmond, VA: International Mission Board.
Garrison, D. (2004). *Church planting movements: how God is redeeming a lost world*. Bangalore, India: WIGTake Resources.
Garrison, D., & Garrison, S. (2008). Factors that facilitate fellowships becoming movements. In J. D. Woodberry (Ed.), *From seed to fruit* (pp. 207-218). Pasadena, CA: William Carey Library.
Gates, A. (1973). Perfection growth. In A. R. Tippett (Ed.), *God, man and church growth* (pp. 128-142). Grand Rapids, MI: Eerdmans.
Glasser, A. (1999). The apostle Paul and the missionary task. In R. D. Winter, S. C. Hawthorne, D. R. Dorr, D. B. Graham, B. A. Koch (Eds.), *Perspectives on the world Christian movement: A reader* (3rd ed.) (pp. 127-134). Pasadena, CA: William Carey Library.
Glover, R. H., & Kane, J. H. (1960). *The progress of world-wide missions* (Rev. ed.). New York, NY: Harper.
Grist, W. A. (1916). *Samuel Pollard: Pioneer missionary in China*. London: Cassell and Company, LTD.
Gupta, P., & Lingenfelter, S. (2006). *Breaking vision to accomplish vision*. Winona Lake, IN: BMH.
Harnack, A. (1961). *The mission and expansion of Christianity*. New York, NY: Harper.
Hawthorne, S. C. (1999). The story of His glory. In R. D. Winter, S. C. Hawthorne, D. R. Dorr, D. B. Graham, B. A. Koch (Eds.), *Perspectives on the world Christian movement: A reader* (3rd ed.) (pp. 34-48). Pasadena, CA: William Carey Library.
Hawthorne, S. C. (2009). *Perspectives on the world Christian movement: The study guide* (4th ed.). Pasadena, CA: William Carey Library.
Hillgarth, J. N. E. (Ed.). (1986). *Christianity and paganism 3650–750 AD: The conversion of western Europe*. Philadelphia: University of Pennsylvania Press.
Hobbs, P. (2012). *Dawn harvest*. Metro Manila: OMF Literature.
Hobbs, P. (2012). *Dawn reapers*. Metro Manila: OMF Literature.
Hodges, M. (1953). *The indigenous church*. Springfield, MO: Gospel Publishing House.
Hong, Y. (2000). Revisiting church growth in Korean Protestantism. *International Review of Mission, 89*(353), 190-202.
Johnson, A. (2009, July–August). Pragmatism, Pragmatism Everywhere! *9 Marks Journal*. Retrieved from http://www.9marks.org/journal/pragmatism-pragmatism-everywhere
Kaiser, W., Jr. (1999). Israel's missionary call. In R. D. Winter, S. C. Hawthorne, D. R. Dorr, D. B. Graham, B. A. Koch (Eds.), *Perspectives on the world Christian movement: A reader* (3rd ed.) (pp. 10-15). Pasadena, CA: William Carey Library.
Keane, W. (2007). *Christian moderns: Freedom & fetish in the mission encounter*. Berkeley: University of California Press
Keysser, C. (1980). *A people reborn*. Pasadena, CA: William Carey Library.
Kraft, C. H. (1979). *Christianity in culture: A study in dynamic biblical theologizing*

in cross-cultural perspective. Maryknoll, NY: Orbis Books.

Kraft, C. H. (2005). SWM/SIS at forty: A participant/observer's view of our history. Pasadena, CA: William Carey Library.

Lee, Y. (2004). The life and ministry of David Yonggi Cho and the Yoido Full Gospel Church. *Asia Journal of Pentecostal Studies, 7*(1), 3-20.

Logan, R. (1989). *Beyond church growth.* Grand Rapids, MI: Baker House Books.

Mallow, P. C. (1998). Khmer leadership: Ancient leadership and current practices. Phnom Penh, Cambodia: World Concern. (In-house report on file in the OMF administrative office in Phnom Penh, Cambodia.).

Mark. (2011a, February 28). Monday is for missiology: Second thoughts on the future of missions [Web log post]. Retrieved from http://edstetzer.com/2011/02/second-thoughts-on-the-future.html

Mark. (2011b, March 6). Re. Monday is for missiology: Second thoughts on the future of missions [Web log comment]. Retrieved from http://www.edstetzer.com/2011/02/second-thoughts-on-the-future.html

McConnell, C. D., ed., (1997). *The Holy Spirit and mission dynamics.* Pasadena, CA: William Carey Library.

McGavran, D. (1955a). *The bridges of God: A study in the strategy of missions.* London: World Dominion Press.

McGavran, D. (2005). *The bridges of God: A study in the strategy of missions.* Eugene, OR: Wipf & Stock Publishers.

McGavran, D. (1955b). *How churches grow.* London: World Dominion Press.

McGavran, D. (1970). *Understanding church growth* (1st. ed.). Grand Rapids, MI: Eerdmans.

McGavran, D. (Ed.). (1972). *Crucial issues in missions tomorrow.* Chicago, IL: Moody Press.

McGavran, D. (1984). *Momentous decisions in missions today.* Grand Rapids, MI: Baker Books.

McGavran, D. A. and Wagner, C. P. (1990). *Understanding church growth.* Grand Rapids, MI: William B. Eerdmans.

McIlwain, T. (1987). *Building on firm foundations vol. 1: Guidelines for evangelism and teaching believers.* Sanford, FL: New Tribes Mission.

McIntosh, G. (2012). *Yearning for growth: The life and ministry of Donald A. McGavran.* Unpublished manuscript.

McPhee, A. (2001). *Pickett's fire: The life, contribution, thought, and legacy of J. Waskom Pickett, Methodist missionary to India.* Wilmore, KY: Asbury Theological Seminary.

McPhee, A. (2002, Fall). Bishop J. Waskom Pickett's rethinking of 1930s missions in India. *International Journal of Frontier Missions, 19*(3), 31-37.

Middleton, V. (1990). *The development of a missiologist: The life and thought of Donald McGavran, 1897-1965.* Pasadena, CA: Fuller Theological Seminary.

Morris, M. (2011, March 7). Re. Monday is for missiology: Second thoughts on the future of missions [Web log comment]. Retrieved from http://www.edstetzer.com/2011/02/second-thoughts-on-the-future.html

Myers, B. (1999). *Walking with the poor.* Maryknoll, NY: Orbis Books.

Neely, Alan. (2000). Missiology. In *Evangelical dictionary of world missions.* Scott

A. Moreau, ed. Pp. 633-635. Grand Rapids, MI: Baker.
Neill, S. (1965). *A history of Christian mission*. London, England: Pelican.
Nevius, J. (1886). *The planting and development of missionary churches*. Nutley, NJ: Presbyterian and Reformed.
Ott, C., & Wilson, G. (2011). *Global church planting: Principles and best practices for multiplication*. Grand Rapids, MI: Baker Academic.
Parsons, G. (2012). *Ralph D. Winter: Early life and core missiology*. Pasadena, CA: WCIU Press.
Patterson, G., & Scoggins, R. (2002). *Church multiplication guide: The miracles of church reproduction*. Pasadena, CA: William Carey Library.
Payne, J. D. (2012). *Roland Allen: Pioneer of spontaneous expansion*. CreateSpace Independent Publishing Platform.
Pickett, J. W. (1933). *Christian mass movements in India*. Lucknow, India: Lucknow.
Pickett, J. W. (1963). *Dynamics of church growth*. Nashville, TN: Abingdon Press.
Pickett, J. W., Warnshius, A. L., Singh, G. H., & McGavran, D. A. (1956). *Church growth and group conversion*. Lucknow, India: Lucknow.
Piper, J. (1999). Let the nations be glad. In R. D. Winter, S. C. Hawthorne, D. B. Graham, B. A. Koch (Eds.), *Perspectives on the world Christian movement: A reader* (3rd ed.) (pp. 49-54). Pasadena, CA: William Carey Library.
Schattner, Frank Walter. *Sustainability Within Church Planting Movements in East Asia*, D.Miss dissertation, Cook School of Intercultural Studies, Biola University, 2013.
Shank, N. (2011, April 10). Re. Monday is for missiology: Second thoughts on the future of missions [Web log comment]. Retrieved from http://www.edstetzer.com/2011/02/second-thoughts-on-the-future.html
Sheffield, H. (1990). *Tribal strategy chart with explanatory notes*. Sanford, FL: New Tribes Mission.
Sills, D. (2010). *Reaching and teaching: A call to great commission obedience*. Chicago IL: Moody Press.
Sire, J. (2004). *Naming the elephant: Worldview as a concept*. Downers Grove, IL: InterVarsity Press.
Smith, S., Kai, Y. (2011). *T4T: A discipleship rerevolution*. Monument, Colorado: WIGTake Resources.
Steffen, T. (1994). Selecting a church planting model that works. *Missiology: An International Review, 12*(3), 365-366.
Steffen, T. (1997). *Passing the baton: Church planting that empowers*. La Habra, CA: Center for Organization and Ministry Development.
Steffen, T. (1998). Flawed evangelism and church planting. *Evangelical Missions Quarterly, 34*(4), 428-435.
Steffen, T. (2005). *Reconnecting God's story to ministry: Crosscultural storytelling at home and abroad*. Donners Grove, IL: IVPress.
Steffen, T. (2011). *The facilitator era: Beyond pioneer church multiplication*. Eugene, OR: WIPF & Stock.
Steffen, T. (2013). Chronological practices and possibilities in the urban world. *Global Missiology*. 2013, 4(10). Retrieved from <http://ojs.globalmissiology.org/index.php/english/issue/view/107>
Stone, B. (2012). *A reader in ecclesiology. (Ashgate contemporary ecclesiology)*.

Burlington, VT: Ashgate Publishing Company.
Stott, J. (1999). The living God is a missionary God. In R. D. Winter, S. C. Hawthorne, D. R. Dorr, D. B. Graham, B. A. Koch (Eds.), *Perspectives on the world Christian movement: A reader* (3rd ed.) (pp. 3-9). Pasadena, CA: William Carey Library.
Taber, Charles R. (2000). *World, to save the world: The interface between missiology and the social sciences.* Harrisburg, PA: Trinity Press International.
Takamizawa, E. (1977). Religious commitment theory: A model for Japanese Christians. *Missiology: An International Review, 5*(2), 203-221.
Taylor, G. (1998). *Behind the ranges: The life-changing story of J. O. Fraser.* Littleton, CO: OMF International.
Tippett, A. (1967). Solomon Islands Christianity: A study in growth and obstruction. London, England: Lutterworth Press.
Tippett, A. R. (1970). *Church growth and the word of God.* Grand Rapids, MI: Eerdmans.
Tippett, A. R. (Ed.). (1973a). *God, man and church growth.* Grand Rapids, MI: Eerdmans.
Tippett, A. R. (1973b). *Verdict theology in missionary theology.* Pasadena, CA: William Carey Library.
Tippett, A. R. (1981). *Church growth and the Word of God: The biblical basis of the church growth viewpoint.* Grand Rapids, MI: William B. Eerdmans Publishing Company.
Tippett, A. R. (1987). *Introduction to missiology.* Pasadena, CA: William Carey Library.
Traveling Team, The. (2013). Glossary of World Christian Terms. [Website]. Retrieved from http://www.thetravelingteam.org/node/195
Vallesky, D. (1990, October 15). The church growth movement: an evaluation. Paper presented to the Ohio Conference, Michigan District, at Our Savior Lutheran Church, Hollidaysburg, PA. Retrieved from http://www.wlsessays.net/files/ValleskeyGrowth.pdf
Wagner, C. P. (Ed.). (1990). *Understanding church growth* (3rd. Rev. ed.). Grand Rapids, MI: Eerdmans.
Walls, A. F. (1990). *The missionary movement in Christian history.* Maryknoll, NY: Orbis Books.
Warneck, G. (1954). *The living Christ and dying heathenism.* Grand Rapids, MI: Baker Books.
Winter, R. (1974). *The highest priority: cross cultural evangelism.* Paper presented at Lausanne 1974, Lausanne, Switzerland. Retrieved from http://www.lausanne.org/docs/lau1docs/0226.pdf
Winter, R. (1999). The mission of the kingdom. In R. D. Winter, S. C. Hawthorne, D. R. Dorr, D. B. Graham, B. A. Koch (Eds.), *Perspectives on the world Christian movement: A reader* (3rd ed.) (pp. 529-530). Pasadena, CA: William Carey Library.
Winter, R. (2009). Three mission eras: And the loss and recovery of mission kingdom. In R. D. Winter, S. C. Hawthorne, D. R. Dorr, D. B. Graham, B. A. Koch (Eds.), *Perspectives on the world Christian movement: A reader* (4th ed.)

(pp. 263-266). Pasadena, CA: William Carey Library.
Wodarz, D. (1979). *Church growth: The missiologist of Donald Anderson McGavran*. Rome, Italy: Pontificia Universitas Gregoriana.
Woodberry, J. D. (Ed.). (2008). *From seed to fruit: Global trends, fruitful practices, and emerging issues among Muslims*. Pasadena, CA: William Carey Library.
Zook, M. (1989). *Church planting step by step*. Sanford, FL: New Tribes Mission Research & Planning.

APPENDIX A
The Wheel: S-CMM
Assessment Tool*
ASSESSING FRUITFUL PRACTICES

Ministry or Team _____

Name of Assessor _____

Fruitful Practice	Progress	Score
Mission	1. No one is taking responsibility for the lost around them. 2. The missionary is taking personal responsibility for the lost around them. 3. The missionary and local leaders are taking personal responsibility for the lost around them. 4. Local leaders and some local believers are taking personal responsibility for the lost around them. 5. Local leaders and the majority of local believers are taking personal responsibility for the lost around them (prayer, abundant gospel sowing).	
Leadership	1. No emerging leaders. 2. Emerging leaders. 3. Outsiders training local leaders but those local leaders are not reproducing themselves. 4. Local leaders taking responsibility to train other leaders in a reproducible way. 5. Leaders emerging and being trained out to the outside edge of the movement.	

APPENDIX A
The Wheel: S-CMM
Assessment Tool*
ASSESSING FRUITFUL PRACTICES

Cont.

Church / Ecclesiology	1. No plan for gathering believers. 2. Believers gathering irregularly but with little understanding of what to do while meeting. 3. Believers gathering semi-regularly with a growing understanding of how to conduct a Christian gathering. 4. Believers meeting weekly, learning to follow the Great Co-mission and the Great Commandment. 5. Believers committed to each other, with a high commitment to the Great Co-mission and Great Commandment as well as following the seven commands of Christ.
Reproduction	1. No plan or commitment to follow 2 Tm. 2:2. 2. Missionary is committed to following 2 Tm. 2:2. 3. 2nd generation of leaders and groups. 4. 3rd generation of leaders and groups plus new streams. 5. 4th generation of leaders and groups plus many new streams. (groups intentionally planting other groups that are multiplying rapidly through multiple streams),=.

APPENDIX A	Cont.
The Wheel: S-CMM Assessment Tool* ASSESSING FRUITFUL PRACTICES	

Worldview Transformation	1. Believers not being systematically taught regularly in a culturally appropriate way. 2. Bible studies prepared and a systematic reproducible plan being used to teach believers in a culturally appropriate way. 3. Outsiders doing systematic teaching of believers addressing worldview and literacy barriers. 4. Local lay leaders teaching local believers emphasizing the authority of the Bible. 5. Believers obeying what they have learned (healthy churches).

KEY: 1-15 = not yet likely of seeing a movement
16-20 = emerging movement
21-25 = on the verge of a sustainable movement

Directions:

This tool with help you assess three very important aspects of your church planting ministry, especially if you would like to see a S-CMM emerge: 1) it will indicate if you are working towards a S-CMM or not, 2) it shows the steps necessary for implementing fruitful practices and where you are on the continuum. It will also show what your next steps are in moving forward towards a movement, and, 3) if your work has plateaued, it identifies which areas must receive focus for the purpose of reigniting the movement.

The WHEEL MODEL

1. You will notice 5 fruitful practices listed along the left column. To the right of each fruitful practice are 5 choices. The choices are listed along a continuum, i.e., #1 = fruitful practice not implemented to #5 = fruitful practice fully implemented.

2. Carefully read each of the 5 options for each fruitful practice in light of your work and pick the option that best describes your ministry. This is your score for that particular fruitful practice and should be written in the box furthest to the right.

3. Repeat step #2 for each fruitful practice.

4. Add up all five scores which represents your total score.

5. Compare your score with the key on the bottom.

If you would like further consultation, feel free to contact Frank Schattner of the Jonathan Project at *faivchoj@comcast.net*